MORALS IN A FREE SOCIETY

Morals in a Free Society

by

Michael Keeling

The Seabury Press · New York

CONTENTS

INTRODUCTION

ANYONE who sets out to write about the practical application of Christian moral ideas in the modern world needs first of all to attempt an answer to three preliminary questions.

1. Does moral language mean anything at all – and if it does, what precisely is the nature of the statements which it makes?

2. How are we to decide what Christian moral ideas are, since Christians are divided and have different views on what constitutes authority?

3. How far can we speak of 'responsibility' at all in the face of psychological, sociological and biological investigations into the causes of human action?

There are no final answers to these questions, but the faith which is a living response to a lively world cannot stand still. The present times are more revolutionary even than those of the Renaissance and the Reformation, and the revolt now is against authority itself. This is in many ways an exciting and encouraging development in human history, though it has its dangers, like any other movement. For the Church it means that its claim to teach now needs to be justified, and that, as in the first days, its authority arises from the quality of the demand which it makes and from the quality of life which it offers; the existential authority of Christ who said: 'I am the bread of life. Whoever comes to me shall never be hungry, and whoever believes in me shall never be thirsty.' Now every statement is examined critically to see if it justifies itself by what it tells us to do, rather than by the fact that it is the Church which says it. Even without this challenge, moral teaching has to change, because sometimes the facts change, and sometimes the way we understand the facts changes. In making moral comments we are really engaged in a very tentative exercise, with both limited knowledge and limited judgement, and the Church as much as any other body needs to be aware of its own fallibility.

It is disturbing to be aware of our own fallibility and we can easily be tempted either to take refuge in an authoritarianism, in 'discipline' and 'standards', or to give up the struggle altogether and lapse into fatalism, apathy, or a desperate search for quick pleasure. Against all these solutions Christianity offers only two watchwords: *tolerance* and *courage*. Tolerance and courage are virtues that have never been absent from the life of Christians in any age (though they have not always been the outward marks of the institutional Church); today they come to the forefront as the most important needs of human society in its present stage, and indeed they have begun to appear already in places where they might least have been expected, as the Second Vatican Council of the Roman Catholic Church has shown.

Tolerance is not a very exciting virtue; it does not sound a battle cry, like 'liberty' or 'equality', but it is none the less very important for the happiness of man. We never pose a greater threat to our fellow human beings than when we want to make them do something, and the better our intentions, the more harm we can effect. Before we set out to change people, there are four conditions that it is as well to be clear about:

1. That we know how to accept people in their present state;

2. that we know that the value of a human being lies in the fact of his existing rather than in the contribution he makes to our idea of Society;

3. that we want the change in order to promote the happiness of the people who must undergo that change rather than to promote our own happiness; and

4. that we can demonstrate the value of the change to the people whom it will affect and not just ask them to take our word for it.

All this demands a great deal more self-restraint and effort to understand other people than we are accustomed to exercise, but what is more difficult is that at the end of such a critical examination of our motives we may be left with many more occasions than we are at present accustomed to, on which we decide that it is not right to try to change people, but that we ought to try to put up with them. This may make demands on us for which we are even less ready.

We therefore need courage as well. Other people are trustworthy because at bottom they are just like ourselves – much more like us, in fact, than we care to admit – and we cannot start to tolerate them until we have begun to tolerate ourselves. It takes courage to trust the universe to be rational and just, and it takes courage to trust other people as equal sharers with ourselves in such a universe. The traditional Christian formulation of the human situation is that God is the

Creator, and humanity is called to be the child of God. The traditional principles that Christianity offers as the basis for action are 'I am acceptable just as I am' and 'All men are acceptable just as they are'. The Church has always tried to work out social practice according to this idea of God and man but without always seeing where it leads, because courage is a commodity that is always in short supply, and Christians like everybody else are children of the age they live in. This is why the attempt has to be made in every generation to reassess what has been said and what should be said with respect for the past, but with respect also for our own ability to see and judge. This book is one such attempt.

NOTE TO THE AMERICAN EDITION

The moral discussion in this book is based on the social facts about one particular society, the United Kingdom (or rather England and Wales, which is the main unit of Britain for purposes of statistics). But the problems of one advanced industrial society are not very different from those of any other, whether we are thinking of economics or whether we are thinking of morals, and when the two societies are Britain and the United States the problems are very much alike. There is poverty in the United States on a scale which is comparable to the poverty in Britain; there is a colour problem in both countries (though in the United States it is larger and has been going longer); the principles of the criminal law are the same in both countries and the principles of economics are the same in both countries. Modern, urban, technological man is the same whether he lives in Detroit (U.S.A.) or in Birmingham (U.K.) – or indeed in Rotterdam or in Yokohama – and the qualities he needs for spiritual and physical survival are the same qualities in each place. This is the justification for offering this book to the American public. On the next page there is a note on statistics relating to the U.S.A., which may enable the reader to make his own translation of the ideas in this book for the American scene.

Comparative Statistics for the United States

Illegitimacy: In the United States, 89,500 illegitimate babies were born in 1940, and the number of illegitimate births has increased each succeeding year until in 1961, out of a total of 4,268,326 live births, 240,200 were illegitimate; and in 1964 there were 275,700 babies born out of wedlock of a total number of 4,027,490 live births. This means that there were over four times as many illegitimate babies born in the United States as in Britain in 1964. But, again, the effect of statistics varies by the way the facts are expressed, and when population figures are taken into consideration and statistics expressed in terms of percentage, the realization is that close to 93 per cent of all births in the United States in 1964 were to married mothers – only a few decimal points' difference from the British percentage.

Although the illegitimate birth rate is also at its highest in the United States for women in their twenties, the peak age is higher than for British women; the largest number of illegitimate births in 1964 were to women between the ages of 25 and 29, and this was true also for 1961. (*Vital Statistics of the United States 1964*, Vol I, U.S. Department of Health, Education and Welfare, Public Health Service, Washington, D.C., 1966.) *Cf.* page 88 in the text.

Divorce: There are similarities in the divorce statistics for the United States, notably the peak period, during which 485,000 divorces were granted in the U.S. in 1945. That figure declined in 1950 to 385,000; there was, however, a slight increase again in 1960 (to 393,000), and in 1962 a further increase to 413,000 divorces granted. (*Statistical Abstract of the United States: 1965*, U.S. Bureau of the Census, Washington, D.C., 1965.) *Cf.* page 91 in the text.

Poverty: Poor families, defined as 'families with total money incomes of less than $3,000 in 1963', number 8,800,000 in the United States. Of these, it is estimated that over 3,000,000 have one to three children under 18 years of age, and 1,000,000 have four or more children. (*Statistical Abstract of the United States: 1965*, U.S. Bureau of the Census, Washington, D.C., 1965.) *Cf.* pages 122-3 in the text.

PART ONE

THEORETICAL CONSIDERATIONS

I

WHAT DO MORAL STATEMENTS MEAN?

THERE is considerable confusion about the implications of the word 'moral'. The most dramatic illustration of this fact on a national level in recent years is provided by an incident in a widely-reported affair in 1963. In the summer of that year a considerable uproar was in progress about certain private activities of the then Secretary of State for War, which were alleged to have put the security of the country to risk, and which, after being first explicitly denied in Parliament, and then admitted, led to the resignation of the Minister. On the eleventh of June, after the Minister's resignation, *The Times* came out with an editorial under the title 'IT *IS* A MORAL ISSUE' in which it was argued that the public had as much right to be concerned about the moral implications of the ex-Minister's actions as about his regard for security: 'Everyone has been so busy assuring the public that the affair is not one of morals, that it is time to assert that it is. Morals have been discounted for too long.' The editorial caused something of a sensation. Many people were pleased and relieved to see in print the assertion that 'morals' (presumably with the implication 'Christian morals') are a matter of common concern. Many more were deeply disturbed by the public invasion of what they regarded as a private matter, and accused *The Times* of reverting to its old game of being the Voice of God. Although both sides were entirely sincere it is very unlikely that the moral principles involved in the affair could be described in a way that would be acceptable to them equally. Those who supported the line of *The Times* editorial would probably say that the belief of former generations that Christian moral ideas are part of the legal and social foundations of British society still holds good; and that a person holding public office must expect to have his private life taken into consideration when his fitness for the work is in question, because his private life reflects upon his powers of judgement generally. Those who opposed the editorial would probably point out that only a small percentage of people in this country are practising Christians; and that all of us – even Ministers of the Crown – have a right to privacy which overrules the right of the public to judge its office holders: public men must be judged by their public acts. Adherence to one view or the other may be a matter of age, politics and social circumstances as much as of moral judgement. *The Times* ran a long subsequent correspondence, but the point was never decided, and never will be: for this, and every other moral question, is a matter of opinion. This is the major difficulty about moral judgements: there is no way of testing them.

Verification

We cannot test statements about morals in the same way that we can test, let us say, statements about temperature; but if we cannot test moral talk by observations with instruments, neither can we verify it by much else. Let us take an example. Suppose we want to test the proposition that 'The highest good for all men is to be found in following the principle, "Love your neighbour as yourself" '.

There is a practical difficulty about testing this by experiment: we cannot cause all men to love their neighbours as themselves for a specified period and then report back. Even to try this out on a small group of people would be unreasonable and impracticable: unreasonable because the hypothesis implies that either the experimental group or the control group would be working on instructions which are wrong, and therefore liable to cause harm and suffering; impracticable because human beings are not identical units to start with, and the task of analysing the results would be insuperably complex. A further practical objection is that we cannot in fact make precise comparisons between the experiences of different people: when two people say 'I am happy', we cannot be sure that they mean the same thing, even if they are deriving their happiness from the same event, such as the birth of their child, or from similar events, such as being on holiday.

There is also a philosophical difficulty about moral statements, arising from the fact that they are set out in a universal and absolute form: we cannot logically test universal statements. Even if we could cause all men to follow our test precept for a specified length of time and then to report back, and even if they all agreed that the experience was a better one than they had ever enjoyed previously, we still could not be sure that we had found the highest good, because there might be lurking somewhere in the infinite a yet better good, waiting to be discovered; and we still could not be sure that the precept would be true for all men, because a future generation, in another experiment, might disagree.

The Way We Use Moral Language

In spite of these difficulties, the practice of passing moral judgements is widespread among the human race and, if we may judge from the amount of time and thought devoted to it, it is an activity to which we attach some value. Some of it admittedly goes no further than keeping the conversation going, but mostly, when we say 'good' or 'bad' or 'right' or 'wrong', we think we are doing something more fundamental than keeping the conversation going, or finding a new way of saying 'I like it' or 'I don't like it'. There are three ways in which our use of moral language suggests that when we make moral judgements we do not think that we are just expressing a personal preference or an emotional reaction.

The first is that when we express a moral view to a fellow human being we generally expect him to share it. The expectation varies according to the person to whom we are talking, but on the whole a man might expect his wife and his employer and his milkman to have similar views over a wide range of moral topics. Even beyond the local community there is an expectation that moral judgements can be exchanged and compared among a wide range of people, and that there is, or ought to be, a common standard of judgement on given questions, such as the rights of property or the taking of human life. When differences of opinion arise, we feel that they matter and ought to be overcome, in a way that we do not feel this about, let us say, differences in our preferences for brands of toothpaste. Moral talk, in other words, sets out to label acts and motives on the assumption that the labels will be understood and accepted by anyone who passes by.

The second way in which our use of moral language suggests that we think that in using moral language we are naming objective qualities, is that most moral systems equate the following of their prescriptions with a person's long-term happiness. Happiness, as we have already remarked, cannot be measured, but there is a commonsense understanding of what it means to say 'I am happy' which is sufficient for our purpose, and in this sense we assume that our moral systems should show results. This means that our moral judgements can to some extent be verified or falsified in action, but it does not contradict the conclusion to which we came in the previous section, namely, that moral statements cannot be proved: the standard of proof which we require for everyday action is quite different from that which we require for philosophical certainty, and while there may be sufficient indications of the truth of a moral statement for us to make up our minds to act or not to act, this does not imply that there is a philosophical proof of its truth or falsity. Moral judgements can therefore be tested in action, but not rigorously.

The third way in which our use of moral language is different from statements of preference or emotion is that our moral judgements assume that a person is free to act. If we think that a particular wrong action is done freely, we may say that the person is wrong in doing it, but if we think that the action is done under compulsion we may not say that the person is wrong. Moral judgements therefore carry with them a particular implication about the nature of man, that a free choice of actions is a possibility for him. It follows that moral statements are limited, so far as they concern the doers of actions, to actions which are done from deliberate choice.

To sum up the argument so far: the way we use moral language suggests that we think that we are making statements which are systematically agreed; which can be tested objectively; and which concern voluntary rather than involuntary actions. These assumptions may be incorrect, but if they are done away with, the whole of our moral language, and the whole possibility of moral language, goes with them.

A Sense of Fitness

From what we have said so far we can dispose of three possibilities about the nature of moral statements: they are not factual statements which anyone can test by observation or experiment; they are not statements about our emotions or preferences; they are not axioms – self-evident truths like those of mathematics and logic – because there is room for dispute about them.

They do, however, resemble axioms in expecting an immediate acceptance, and the definition to which they come nearest is perhaps that of 'intuitions' (*see* Sir W. David Ross, *Foundations of Ethics*, London: Oxford University Press, 1949). An intuition is defined in *The Concise Oxford Dictionary* as an 'immediate apprehension by the mind without reasoning'; it is like an axiom in that it is perceived directly, but it does not necessarily need to be accepted by all reasoning men in order to have validity for the person who perceives it. An intuition also stands to be checked by the way it works in daily life, but we do not have to check the way it works before we decide to act upon it, and we may be willing to continue to act upon it even when there is evidence against it.

Instead of a direct intuition of our own we may act upon principles we receive from a moral system, religious or otherwise, but even here the perception that we ought to act upon these principles is our own. There is no difference in terms of rationality between holding moral ideas from a revealed religion and holding them from any other source: either way the questions which arise are 'Do these ideas seem to me to be good?' and 'Do these ideas work?'. Beliefs held by revelation are still liable to be questioned if they do not work out in life, while ideas held initially by the exercise of reason can become deeply entrenched against the possibility of questioning. Whether or not we remain open-minded is a question not of the origin of our ideas but of our own honesty and humility.

The whole question of our principles of action might be tackled from the other end, so that instead of comparing existing moral codes we might set out to discover from scratch, by sociological investigation, what rules of conduct would be most helpful and practical in our society; but this does not eliminate the moral problem, which is that of choosing what sort of a society we want. Sociology is a method of study, and it does not select our goals for us. As soon as we begin to investigate what we mean by 'practical' and 'helpful', and ask 'practical for whom?' and 'helpful to what end?' we are back with those questions about the nature of man and of society which are the concern of moral systems.

In making moral judgements there is no fixed relationship between what we should believe and what we should prove. The three elements of moral activity are our beliefs about the nature of man and of the world, our estimates of the practical effects of our possible actions, and our freedom to choose to act. The distinctive nature of a moral judgement is that it is about actions which we freely choose to do, conceiving them to have a direct relationship to the way the world is made, so that it matters which way we choose. In this sense 'right' and 'wrong' are absolutes, because the world is made in only one way; but because we cannot attain to philosophical certainty that any particular choice is 'right' or 'wrong', the authority of a moral statement made by anyone else depends on its direct appeal to our own intuition – the extent to which we feel that it fits in with our own understanding of the way the world is made (including the possibility that such a moral statement may open up to us a new sense of fitness, or new possibilities of action) – and on what we know of the person who makes it and of the sort of life it seems to have produced in him. The only valid form for a moral statement which we ourselves make is 'I think' – or 'I believe' – 'that this is right' and the only way of testing it, in the end, is to do it.

The position therefore is that we have to make moral decisions; that moral decisions are essentially decisions about the fitness or harmony of actions with our own nature and that of the whole world (or in Christian terms with the nature of God); and that when all the arguments have been added up, this fitness or harmony is something which we perceive directly, by a process which we have called intuition, but which also in traditional ethical discussion has the name 'conscience'.

Moral Statements and Scientific Statements

How should we rate morals as a study? The fact that moral judgements vary widely, and that they depend on intuition rather than experiment, might seem to reduce the usefulness of ethics as a serious study, but there are two things to be said in its defence.

The first is that ethics has the same standing as any other 'arts' subject: all the studies whose subject-matter involves the voluntary behaviour of human beings are up against the problem of inconsistency and unpredictability, and ethics shares its difficulties with aesthetics, economics, psychology and sociology. Presumably no one would suggest writing off all these subjects.

The second is that even the experimental sciences are dependent to some extent on the workings of intuition. An example of this was given by the Professor of Botany at the University of Southampton in a talk on the B.B.C., in which he described how, in the course of some work on the ecology of Denny Wood in the New Forest, after various difficulties he hit on a method of analysing the data which produced important practical results, but for which he lacked a formal proof. Indeed, he was assured by two people there, as he said:

> The quantities I had calculated could not be added in this offhand way; the process would be invalid and the results meaningless. The trouble was that it worked. And so I had to think again. After much thinking I came up with a

story: if I added, not the values themselves but their square roots, I could pretend that what I was doing was a crude approximation to another, and reasonably respectable, process known as factor analysis. The argument was, frankly, tortuous and not convincing; but it was all I had and it had to do.[1]

The method which Professor Williams invented was used on other data, and by research teams in other subjects, but it was not until some years later that he was given from two independent sources a proof that his original method of calculation was able to do what he knew it could be done in practice. He commented:

But how does one instinctively arrive at a correct answer? We usually explain such things by supposing that our subconscious minds go to work on the problem and then come up with the result when they are ready. But this will not do. Both the proofs I had been given involved statistical knowledge I did not possess (and, for that matter, still do not): and so neither of them was available to my subconscious mind. This is the way it goes with most ideas in scientific research. They just come to you from nowhere, as themes come to a composer. The comparison is a good one, since many scientists are amateur musicians. And scientists differ quantitatively among themselves in much the same way as composers. In the days when key-signatures were still popular, Tchaikovsky, Grieg, Dvorak, Elgar could all pour out memorable tunes – as, in later and more frivolous fields, could Coward, Gershwin and Kern. But other composers are now remembered by only a single tune. Great scientists throw off new ideas all the time; the rest of us have one, now and then.[2]

The experimental sciences resemble the moral sciences also in having suffered from the distortions which arise when the observer is involved with his subject in such a way that he may wish to prejudge his conclusions. In morals the result of coming to a particular set of conclusions may be far-reaching and even painful (what happens to a man who decides that the saying, 'Sell your possessions, and give to the poor, and then you will have riches in heaven; and come, follow me', is one that he ought to take literally?); in science the result may be less dramatic and less direct, but people will still depart quite a long way from reason and from proof in the interests of their self-respect and of their reputations. Sir William Macewen commented on the reception accorded to the ideas of Pasteur and Lister: 'The new treatment, and the theory on which it was founded, were received at first – save by a few faithful pupils – with scepticism and coldness,

[1] W. T. Williams, 'The Computer Botanist', *The Listener*, 12 December, 1963, pp. 983–5.
[2] *Ibid.*

and later with open hostility. . . . The usual fate meted out to innovators or disturbers of settled doctrines was shared by Lister.'³ Macewen himself met with the same hostility within the medical profession in pursuing the teaching of Lister; it came often from men who were as highly qualified as the innovators themselves, and as much concerned with and distressed by the problem of the mortality rate in surgical cases. The difference between the sciences and morals is that scientific means of verification ensure that a new technique can in the end impose itself, but in morals the argument can go on, and does.

The Validity of Moral Systems

There is no moral system that can claim the right to be enforced on all men. Moral ideas are valid only for those who hold them, and if a moral idea were shared by every person in the world but one, it could not be morally binding on that one man. He might of course be compelled by the rest of us to conform to our moral ideas for the sake of our (or his) safety and of public order, but it would not then be our superior morals that triumphed, but our superior force.

The dilemma of morals is that the ultimate guarantee of our moral system (whatever it may be) is no more than our own personal perception. If it be admitted that moral ideas concern the structure of the universe, rather than simple personal preference, we can then claim that some moral ideas must be right and others wrong, but we have no way of showing conclusively that our own moral perceptions are the right ones. For the sake of living together at all we have to have laws and agreements, but a knowledge of the nature of our moral judgements should make us very cautious indeed about legislating in matters of morals, or wanting to make other men be good. 'Moral indignation' has a good righteous sound about it, but 'tolerance' and 'humility' may be closer to the nature of God.

³ A. K. Bowman, *The Life and Teaching of Sir William Macewen* (London: Hodge, 1942), p. 54.

2

THE SOURCES OF
CHRISTIAN MORAL JUDGEMENTS

WE have already mentioned in general terms two sources of moral judgement: *intuition*, which is our apparent capacity to arrive spontaneously at moral opinions, and *revelation*, which concerns the receiving or deducing of specific moral principles from religious belief. Whether we accept a religious revelation or not, some moral ideas are fed into our intuition from outside, possibly from a philosophical system which does not come under the heading of religion, but certainly from our parents, our teachers and our friends, and from social influences generally. This input is used in different ways by different people, some of it being accepted, some rejected, and some accepted in a modified form. Part of the business of religious and other moral systems is to counteract at least some of the ideas we have received from other sources; whether this is a good thing or a bad thing depends on how we value the system concerned. The time has come, therefore, when we must leave the general discussion of morals, and turn to a consideration of the Christian moral system.

Christian moral ideas come from three main sources: *the Bible*, which is 'revelation' or 'things shown'; *the Church*, which is the whole body of Christians, not only the present generation but also to some extent past – and to some extent future – generations; and *conscience*, which is the term used in traditional moral theology for what we have been calling 'intuition', and which draws on what our minds can make out of the world around us, as well as on the other sources of moral information that we have mentioned. These three sources we shall consider in detail, but first there is a preliminary question lying in our way: namely, is the belief which the Christian religion requires a barrier to the rational discussion of moral issues?

Reason and Belief

Belief in God involves an act of intellectual submission to this extent: that we admit the world to be a bigger affair than reason can sort out by itself. This is not a matter of questions which science has not yet got round to answering, but of questions which by their nature science is incapable of answering – the fundamental questions of purpose, both for the universe as a whole, and for ourselves in daily life. To allow a limit to what reason can do is not unreasonable. In daily life a great deal of our experience involves emotion and intuition rather than reason, and we are the richer for it; reason does not write poetry, nor fall in love, nor bring up children – which does not make us irrational beings, but it does show that reason is not the only mode of experience open to us, nor even necessarily the judge of our experiences. What is true of literature and of love is true also of believing in God. To admit the reality of the supernatural is to open a further possibility of experience, without reducing the value of reason itself. It also might be said that whether we choose to believe or whether we choose not to believe we are equally outside the realm of reason; the one choice is not more rational than the other, because to disbelieve in God is to believe in the supremacy of reason, which is equally unproven. Both choices are a leap in the dark, and both sides may claim to act with intellectual integrity.

For those who choose to believe, the full possibilities of criticism, of argument and of the search for further truth remain, and the answers are not given in advance: the proper form for a statement of belief is not 'I believe for ever' but 'I believe at this moment'. What maintains a Christian in his belief is not that his mind is closed to other possibilities, but that he finds that his religion works. It is the daily experience of the effect of his belief in action (as well as the direct experience of the presence of God) that enables the Christian to raise questions on human reason itself and make it answer for what it says – and sometimes to resist what seems 'reasonable' because what seems 'good' is equally strong. In fact the Christian, relying on the present work of the Spirit rather than on particular formulations of belief, may be in a more open-ended situation than the rationalist philosopher relying on his own arguments.

The Bible

The authority of the Bible, like the authority of the Christian religion, is derived from the fact that it works. Being a very complex book, it has parts which are of less value than others, but the interesting thing about the Bible as a whole is how well it stands up to criticism. The stories of the creation and of Adam and Eve are often used as examples of the fact that the Bible is short on scientific knowledge (which is true of all ancient writings), but even a brief examination of them shows that they still retain their value for their original purpose, which is to make moral and theological statements about the world we live in and the sort of people we are. The aim of the creation story (Gen. 1.1–2.3) is to teach that the whole material universe has come into being by God's will, and is entirely upheld by him. In the history of ideas the account of creation given by Genesis is important for its rejection of the idea of competing and equally powerful gods of light and darkness, and for its rejection of extravagant explanations of the origin of the various features of the material world. There is considerable economy in its statements about light and darkness, sea and land, rain and streams, and plant and animal life (*see* the discussion 'Creation' between Anthony Flew and D. M. MacKinnon in *New Essays in Philosophical Theology*, London, SCM Press, 1955).

The story of Adam and Eve sets out to explain the nature of evil; it is not an historical or theological account of the origin of evil, but a firm and lucid account of the self-destroying nature of self-regarding action (Gen. 3.1–4.10). The story begins with the serpent, which is at once an acknowledgement of the fact that the origin of evil is not open to explanation (the serpent is already there in the garden), and that there is more harm abroad in the world than can be explained by man's action alone. The temptation which is put before the man and the woman is to set themselves up – the serpent promises 'ye shall be as God' – which, under the name of 'pride' or 'ambition' or 'the exercise of reason', is the idea that humanity, and this human being in particular, is the high point of the universe, and the point of reference for everything else. The man and the woman eat the fruit which the serpent offers, and at once find that there is a price to be paid for what they have done: if men are not really 'as God' the attempt to live as if they were must create a strain, and the strain shows first in the most intimate (and therefore the most vulnerable) relationship, the sexual relationship: shame enters in and 'they knew that they were naked'.

Shame about sexual relations is a mark of fear, and fear is the product of immaturity: we know too much to have the freedom of innocence, but we have not yet won through to the freedom of complete self-knowledge and self-acceptance. Called to account by God, man passes from pride to betrayal: 'the woman whom thou gavest to be with me, she gave me of the tree, and I did eat'. In George Orwell's *1984* the final breaking point for Winston comes when the interrogator O'Brien brings him to beg that his lover should suffer the torture which he cannot face himself: when truth is the first victim, love is the second. In two more stages the effects become wider and deeper: firstly, man finds that his life on earth is 'cursed' and all his relationships are affected, even the way he uses the soil – 'in toil shalt thou eat of it all the days of thy life'; secondly, in what is really a separate story, but arising out of the story of the Fall, the breakdown of human relationships is pressed to its logical conclusion: the two uses of the soil conflict and Cain the ploughman murders Abel the herdsman, offering the justification that has stalked mankind through the ages – 'Am I my brother's keeper?' What began in breaking the real order of life by exalting the 'I' at the expense of God ends in the breaking even of elementary human order, by the exaltation of the 'I' at the expense of another man. The 'I' can grow only at the expense of the other, and reduces him finally to the status of a thing to be used.

Professor Hoyle, at the end of his book *The Nature of the Universe*, asks: 'Is it in any way reasonable to suppose that it was given to the Hebrews to understand mysteries far deeper than anything we can comprehend, when it is quite clear that they were completely ignorant of many matters that seem commonplace to us?'[1] The question, of course, is not a logical one, since there is no necessary connection between the states of advancement of different areas of knowledge, nor is scientific method the only way of understanding mysteries; but the direct answer is to look at what the Hebrews actually said about the mysteries of human existence, and on this evidence their understanding of the workings of human relationships and of the moral nature of the universe is as profound as that of any modern philosopher or scientist. Whether or not the stories are literally true is a question that would probably have had no meaning for the Hebrews: what mattered then and what matters now is that when the stories are translated into everyday life they work, because the underlying

[1] Fred Hoyle, *The Nature of the Universe* (Oxford: Blackwell, 1957), p. 109.

analysis is sound. It is from this fact that the Old Testament derives its authority.

The New Testament has a different authority, because it is primarily eyewitness to a man. Even in the Epistles, which are more concerned with teaching and advice than with events, we find John giving his credentials as those of an eyewitness: 'It was there from the beginning; we have heard it; we have seen it with our own eyes; we looked upon it, and felt it with our own hands; and it is of this we tell' (I John 1.1). Paul was similarly concerned to establish his claim to the status of eyewitness, through his vision on the Damascus road; the first two chapters of his letter to the Galatians are largely taken up with this point. The authority of the New Testament, therefore, depends on three things. First of all, it gives us an impression of the man Jesus, who he was and what he did, and if it conveys any authority at all, it is that which the man from Nazareth had for the people who listened to him. Secondly, we want to know about the quality of the eyewitnesses themselves – what sort of people were these men, and what effect did the events which they describe have on them? Are the human qualities which come to us through their writings consistent with the story which they told? Thirdly, there is the authority which arises from what the New Testament does to our own lives: does it create in us new ways of seeing the world, and new ways of acting in it? The New Testament continues the work of the Old in the analysis of what men are and of what the world is, and it opens to us a way of acting that will satisfy ourselves and not hurt others: but its authority we can test only by trying it.

As we have already said, not all parts of the Bible are of equal value. The story of Elisha in which she-bears attacked forty-two children who had been mocking him may have a typological significance, but it seems a severe way of inculcating respect for the prophet (II Kings 2.23–4). Some parts of the Old Testament are superseded by the ideas of the New Testament, and some of both the Old and New Testaments are of significance more for the time in which they were written than for our own; but even those parts of the Old Testament which are superseded by New Testament teaching sometimes represented a moral advance in themselves: the injunction 'An eye for an eye, and a tooth for a tooth' (Matt. 5.38, cited from Ex. 21.24) was a means of limiting revenge rather than of encouraging it. When all the passages are taken into account which may be considered questionable either from the point of view of their origin or from the

point of view of their teaching, they do not constitute any challenge
either to the Christian understanding of life or to the authority of the
Bible, in the sense in which we have defined that authority here.

There is one more caution to be set down: even the Bible does not
give a complete account of God. It gives a sufficient account, but it
is not the whole truth; the final way of knowing God is the way of
unknowing, of the direct penetrating of the spirit inwards to the
living presence, without intervention of words or images:

All things whatsoever that can be thought in the heart or told with the
tongue, or seen with the eyes, or touched with the hands – all are as naught
in respect of, and in comparison with, those things that cannot be thought, nor
seen, nor touched. All the saints and all the sages that have passed away, and
all those that are in this present life, and all that shall come after us, that spake
or wrote, or that shall speak or write, of God, ne'er told nor e'er can tell of
God so much as a grain of millet would be in respect of, or in comparison with,
the heavens and the earth, nay, even a thousand thousandfold less. For all
scripture that speaketh of God, speaketh of Him with stammering voice, as
the mother doth who prattles with her child, that could not understand her
words if she spoke in other fashion.[2]

The Mind of the Church

There was a time when the young Church had to make a crucial
decision about what was to be required in the way of religious obser-
vance from converts who were not Jews, and the whole future of
Christianity hung upon the answer: if the Apostles had decided in
favour of the law of Moses, the possibility of converting the non-
Jewish world would have been negligible. A meeting was held in
Jerusalem of the leaders of the Church at which the problem was
stated, together with much argument on both sides; there was a strong
plea for freedom from Peter, and an account of the work among the
Gentiles from Barnabas and Paul. At the end the decision was made
not to impose the law of Moses on the new Christians. In the letter
which was sent out to the Christians of Antioch, Syria and Cilicia,
the ruling was given in this formula: 'It is the decision of the Holy
Spirit, and our decision, to lay no further burden upon you beyond
these essentials . . .' (Acts 15.28). This is the key to the Christian
community's understanding of itself as a source of moral authority,
that it believes that it is a people through whom the Spirit works.

[2] 'Sayings of Friar Giles,' *The Little Flowers of St Francis* (London: Dent, 1963)
p. 156.

The expectation of the Christian community is that it is the will of God that will prevail, if the Church is patient, and willing to listen, and trying honestly to know what God wants. The will of God is expressed through what the whole Christian community thinks – what is technically called 'the mind of the Church' – and it is shown primarily in ways of worship and ways of living, and only secondarily in the decisions of councils, and in doctrines and creeds. Although it takes a long time to express itself, working through the consciences and worship of a vast number of people, it is, in the end, what directs the Church in all its parts – even those parts which seem to have a framework that leaves no room for it.

This process of decision-making is not to be confused with decisions taken through any particular organ or institution. At any time a given man or body of men can make a wrong decision, and it may take a very long time – even centuries – for the question to be worked through, but the Christian belief is that in the end there will emerge a consensus which will correct the mistake. The concept of 'the mind of the Church' has been developed more fully in eastern Christendom than in the west, and one of the best descriptions of its nature and operation comes from Maurice Villain, in the chapter 'Spiritual Approaches to Orthodoxy' in his book *Unity*. Although the Orthodox are divided into five independent patriarchates, Villain says: 'Let us be quite clear: it is the Orthodox Church, in the singular, although its different branches are autocephalous. It has a real unity.'[3] The way in which this unity works in the Orthodox Church is the model of all Christian decision-making:

... the authority of the Orthodox Church is not outside and above the faithful; it belongs to the whole Church, which is life in Christ under the guidance of the Spirit; it is an integral part of the Church. This idea is expressed in the one Russian word, *sobornost*, which is almost untranslatable.

Let me try to explain it. The term *sobor* means 'council' or 'gathering of the Church' (it is the equivalent of *synodos*). The noun *sobornost*, which is derived from it, means 'conciliarity'. The Orthodox Church is called the 'conciliar' Church (*sobornaia*), the Church which gathers and unites, and it is by this adjective that the Slav creed translates the word καθολική in the Greek creed. 'I believe in the Catholic Church', sings the Greek; 'I believe in the conciliar Church', sings the Russian. It should be noted, by the way, that 'catholicity' in this sense puts the accent not on the *quantitative* or geographical element, but on the qualitative element; on the Church's capacity for totality

[3] Maurice Villain, *Unity* (London: Harvill Press, 1953), p. 151.

vis-à-vis the revealed truth, which must be proclaimed universally, and *vis-à-vis* every man, who must be won for God; also on the capacity of each part to reflect the Whole. Our (*sc. Roman Catholic*) theologians agree in recognising that this point of view is in fact a primordial one.

The *sobornost* is, in some sort, the Church's subconscious – or better still, its superconscious; it is the Church's intimate experience of its own life, as a result of which it knows that it is full of the Spirit and Truth. It belongs to all, clergy and laity, and this is what constitutes, properly speaking, the authority of the Church.

To sum up, authority is not retained by the hierarchical body alone, as if by an element above the mass of the faithful; it is inside the Church as a whole, and consequently richer than any doctrinal utterance by the hierarchy, richer even than any pronouncement signed by the council, since, to be accurate, it is ineffable. No one is in a position to pass judgement on the intimate 'conciliarity' of the Church; it is the 'conciliarity' which judges everything, including the ecumenical council itself, since it is, in some sort, superior to the council.

But this does not mean that there is no teaching authority: it goes without saying that the council has a normative value in everyone's view, and everyone regards it as infallible in practice. Nevertheless, the meaning is that authority cannot simply be imposed from above; it must first emanate from within.[4]

Natural Law

Apart from the Bible and the Church we receive moral ideas from other sources which are not specifically Christian. Traditional moral philosophy holds that there exist general rules of cause and effect in human behaviour which reflect the way in which the world is made, and which can be grasped by anyone who wants to understand them. On this view there is a moral law of the universe which predicts that certain actions will lead to happiness or unhappiness in something of the same way that physical law predicts that water will tend to run down hill rather than up. This system of cause and effect in human behaviour is called the 'natural law'. Paul has the same point in mind (although 'law' for him means specifically the Mosaic law of the Old Testament) when he says: 'When Gentiles who do not possess the law carry out its precepts by the light of nature, then, although they have no law, they are their own law, for they display the effect of the law inscribed on their hearts' (Rom. 2.14). Moral philosophers may be wrong about this natural law, but if it does not exist – if the world does not have a moral structure – then it is impossible to use the

[4] *Ibid.*, pp. 159–60.

words 'good', 'bad', 'right' and 'wrong' in a way that means anything at all, and it is impossible to predict the consequences of any
action in terms of joy, sorrow, peace or regret. If, on the other hand,
a system of moral cause and effect does exist, it must be fairly easy to
discover, otherwise we limit the possibility of good action to philosophers. This means that there should be a great many moral ideas in
common between those who are Christians and those who have other
beliefs – which indeed there are. It means also that the world itself,
and the way we behave in it, can tell us something about God, and
that the moral ideas of Christians, as much as those of anyone else,
have to be tested against the way the world actually is. As Dorothy
Sayers wrote in *The Mind of the Maker*:

It is idle to complain that a society is infringing a moral code intended to make
people behave like St Francis of Assisi if the society retorts that it does not
wish to behave like St Francis, and considers it more natural and right to
behave like the Emperor Caligula. When there is a genuine conflict of opinion,
it is necessary to go behind the moral code and appeal to the natural law – to
prove, that is at the bar of experience, that St Francis does in fact enjoy a
freer truth to essential human nature than Caligula, and that a society of
Caligulas is more likely to end in catastrophe than a society of Franciscans.[5]

We come across the natural law in the way other people treat us,
and how we feel in consequence; in the way we treat other people,
and what we can gather about the way they feel in consequence; and
in our general observation of the world. Along with the teaching of
experience we receive a number of moral ideas directly from parents
and teachers and friends which we hold untested by experience; and
even some of the ideas which we think we have tested by experience
may be inaccurate because they have been deduced wrongly, or
deduced from insufficient data. Our moral ideas, therefore, are an
amalgam of the tested and the untested, the workable and the unwork-
able, the true and the false. The process by which we select the moral
ideas we intend to apply, and resolve conflicts of ideas, and decide
whether our ideas have worked or not, is what we call 'conscience'.

Conscience

Conscience, which we have also called 'intuition', is our ability to

[5] Dorothy Sayers, *The Mind of the Maker* (London: The Religious Book Club,
1942), p. 8.

take moral terms and apply them to our own actions and those of other people.

There is a principle of reflection in men, by which they distinguish between, approve and disapprove their own actions. We are plainly constituted such sort of creatures as to reflect upon our own nature. The mind can take a view of what passes within itself, its propensions, aversions, passions, affections, as respecting such objects and in such degrees; and of the several actions consequent thereupon. In this survey it approves of one, disapproves of another, and towards a third is affected in neither of these ways, but is quite indifferent. This principle in man, by which he approves or disapproves his heart, temper, and actions, is conscience; for this is the strict sense of the word, though sometimes it is used so as to take in more.[6]

When everything else has been said, we have to trust our own judgement; even when it is a question of whether or not our own judgement is wrong, we remain the only people who can decide the question to our own satisfaction. It is important to note again the fundamental assumption of morals that we do decide freely for or against an action. The value we place upon the free exercise of conscience is a measure of the value we place upon the individual human being: the more highly we value each person because he exists as a human being, the more highly we will value his right to make his own moral choices. If we look at life from a Christian point of view, freedom of conscience becomes more rather than less important, because Christianity values highly (more highly, perhaps, than any other religion does) the individual human being, and because the individual, like the Christian community, in seeking to know what is right is co-operating with the Spirit, which is the fundamental activity of human life.

Our conscience is not, of course, infallible, any more than any other moral source. Our moral judgements vary because of the different sorts of programme that can be fed into our conscience, as well as because we are freely making different moral choices; among the factors which decide our actions are some inaccurate moral ideas, and some desires other than the desire for moral good. It is not difficult to give an air of moral righteousness to something that we want to do for quite different reasons. Consequently, even the fact that we think something is 'right' is not an absolute indication that it is right, even for ourselves, and our judgement of others is not necessarily correct, even on our own moral terms.

[6] Joseph Butler, 'Upon Human Nature,' *Fifteen Sermons* (London: Bell, 1952). para. 8.

Conclusion

There are several sources from which we can draw our moral ideas. The Bible has moral authority so far as the Old Testament is concerned by reason of the accuracy of its analysis of human relationships and the moral order of the world, and so far as the New Testament is concerned by reason of its being eyewitness to Jesus of Nazareth; but it does not lay down precise rules for our present action, and it needs careful interpretation. The Church is the community within which the Spirit works, and it is the community within which the response to Jesus and the work of analysis are carried on; but the day-to-day decisions of the Christian community are not infallible (although those decisions which have held good for a very long time for the whole body of Christians have a very strong presumption in their favour). Conscience draws on the Bible and on the Church, on what we can perceive of the natural law, and on the ideas of the people around us, and it verifies its ideas in action; but even conscience is not entirely to be trusted, because some of the ideas that have been fed into it are not reliable, and some of the deductions we have made are incorrect (each of us has only a limited willingness to make right moral choices).

We follow conscience because we must, but we have an obligation to Christian authority (that is, to the Bible and to the Church) not to go against them unless we are deeply convinced of the need to act, and even then only if we are deeply convinced that the harm which will result from not acting is very much greater than the harm which will result from acting. On the other hand, 'authority' has an obligation towards us, not to require of us anything but that which is essential to the maintenance of the fellowship: that we should confess that 'Jesus is Lord', that we should break bread together, and that we should try to act in love. There is more to the Christian religion than this, but this is what makes a man 'a Christian'.

There is no single Christian code, and there is nowhere that the Christian – or anyone else for that matter – can turn for simple and infallible moral advice. It would be tempting to take refuge in a single authority and a clear moral code, but it would be a false solution. In reality we live in a state of tension between (1) what we think we want, (2) what people tell us we ought to want, and (3) what in the unchanging purpose of God we do want. Fortunately on some matters these three versions of reality point to the same answer, but on other they do not, and we have to live with the tension between them, as best we can (until we resolve it by coming to understand something of the being of God, but that goes beyond the making of moral choices).

Tension is an uncomfortable thing to live with, but the difficulty which it causes is a great deal more desirable than the harm which comes from enforcing a false certainty. People who have been very certain of the truth they wanted to enforce include the Inquisition, the Bolsheviks, the National Socialists and the Close Brethren. Paul, on the other hand, was very certain of what he believed, but very concerned also about respect for the needs of others. To admit the possibility of doubt about our moral choices at least leaves open the possibility of new vision and a fresh grasp of the truth. It also calls for courage. The simple solution of opting for the Church or the Bible calls for courage of one sort: the courage of desperate action, which has made martyrs in the past, and led to much good; but the complex solution of looking for the truth with an open mind and standing upon our own responsibility to make decisions calls for courage of a different sort: the courage of humility and of accepting what may seem a threat to personality itself – the courage of not knowing. This is the courage of Christ in Gethsemane – 'Father, if it be thy will, take this cup away from me. Yet not my will but thine be done'; and again, on the cross, 'My God, my God, why has thou forsaken me?' – against the courage of his followers: 'Lord, shall we use our swords?'

The only moral absolute is the being of God, and all our teaching is only an approach to the knowledge of God; it should be accepted for the tentative stuff that it is. Moral codes we must have, because it is not practical to work out every question from the beginning for ourselves, but to use them safely we have to remember that more important than our code is the working of the Spirit: 'The wind blows where it wills; you hear the sound of it, but you do not know where it comes from, or where it is going. So with everyone who is born from Spirit' (John 3.8).

3

HUMAN RESPONSIBILITY

THERE was a woman in New York (so a news item not so very long ago alleged) who, being brought before a court for failing to keep her dog under proper control, answered with evidence from a 'dog psychiatrist' that the animal was suffering from a psychological disturbance and was therefore not responsible for its actions. The psychiatrist William Sargent, in an article in *New Society* based on a paper he gave to the British Association in 1965 says:

The four basic temperaments described by Hippocrates a thousand years before Christ are also still recognisable. Pavlov, after 20 years of patient observation and experimentation with dogs, even came to the conclusion that the four main temperaments of his dogs were the same as the Hippocratic temperaments in man. Once we realise that differences in basic human personality types are mainly due to our genetic inheritance and not, as some psychiatrists have led us to believe, largely to the result of childhood experiences, then it will become much easier to understand the varieties of behaviour and thought that can occur in different people being given exactly the same drugs.[1]

The extension of psychiatry from human beings to dogs represents one extreme in the explanation of behaviour, and the drawing of parallels between personality types and genetical inheritance in human beings and in dogs is perhaps another. Even leaving out the dogs, and ignoring for the moment the question of divisions between different schools of psychiatry, the explanations of human behaviour which are now being produced in various fields of study are tending to

[1] William Sargent, 'Drugs and the Mind,' *New Society*, 30 December, 1965, pp. 8–12. As frequent use is made of quotations from *New Society*, it is worth remarking that in a general magazine of this nature results cannot be reported with the same fulness and rigour that are possible in a specialized journal, but that the articles are of great value as an indication of the sort of investigation that is going on in various fields.

B

make inroads on the concept of 'responsibility', which is the foundation of all moral ideas. There is as yet insufficient agreement on the total explanation of human behaviour for general comments to be of much use, and a detailed study of the findings of such disciplines as sociology, economics, education, psychology, animal behaviour and genetics is beyond the scope of this book. All we can do, therefore, is to indicate briefly the directions in which these studies, or some of them, are working and the implications which they may have in the long run for the concept of human responsibility.

Intentions and Consequences

There is one general point about the concept of responsibility which makes it impossible for us ever to say simply 'We are responsible for our actions'. This is the fact that we may not foresee, or intend, all the consequences which actually follow from what we do.

The person who started the fire in Pudding Lane which burned down the greater part of the city of London in 1666 is unlikely to have intended to devastate the whole town; whoever it was cannot be held to have been entirely responsible for the Great Fire. Many of the things which we do have accidental or unforeseen consequences; there may be a sense in which we ought to have foreseen them, and would have done if we had taken a little more time for thought or a little more trouble to inform ourselves, and to that extent we are responsible even for the unforeseen consequences, but in general there is a limit to our power to foresee and therefore to our responsibility.

The other possibility is that we may know that undesirable consequences will follow from our action, but we do not intend them in the sense of wanting them to happen for their own sake. I think it would be true to say that by and large Britain went to war in 1939 without in any way desiring the deaths of those, both British and German, who were to be killed in the fighting. How far were the British 'responsible' for those who died? We cannot say 'Not at all', because there was an alternative course open to the British people – unconditional surrender – which would have avoided nearly all the deaths; but we cannot say 'Fully responsible' because Britain would probably not have gone to war if the Germans had stayed within their own frontiers (though some would argue that conditions within Germany, like conditions within South Africa now, ought to have led us to military action).

Although this sort of question limits our responsibility, there are no circumstances in which we can entirely avoid the responsibility for an action voluntarily undertaken which causes harm to others, however good our primary aim may be. This is important because a great deal of harm can come from the side effects of an action which has quite a good main intention, and we have to be quite sure that we are ready to bear all the consequences of what we do before we act (even if some of those consequences arise because of what other people have done). For example, we may decide to remove a child from his family for his own protection, and put him in the care of a 'fit person' (such as a local authority children's home); and we may say, 'It is the fault of the mother and father, who are bad parents', but nevertheless it is we who have taken the child out of the family. Possibly we had no alternative, but just possibly more thought, more effort, and more expenditure might have produced a different solution, and for this reason if for no other we must not allow ourselves to shuffle off responsibility for the actions we undertake. We obviously do in some sense 'intend' any consequence which we know will follow from an action if we are still determined, in spite of that knowledge, to carry it out.

The fact that unforeseen and unintended consequences mitigate our responsibility a little, even if they cannot entirely remove it, produces a gap between what happens (the harm or the good that is done) and the amount of responsibility (or 'guilt', or 'merit') that we can allocate to particular people in connection with the happening. Sometimes the 'remainder' can be attributed to known groups such as 'Germany' or 'the child's parents' (though further analysis of the causes of the actions of Germany or the child's parents would show another gap), but often there are so many factors involved that we cannot blame anyone, or any group, for the whole of the hurt that is caused. When we come to consider other factors which mitigate responsibility, such as the arguments of psychologists and others about the causes of human behaviour, we are left with a substantial gap between the amount of suffering present in the world and the responsibility of particular individuals for causing it. (There may also be a similar gap concerning the amount of happiness present in the world – if we may speak in these quantitative terms – but that receives less attention.) There is a natural tendency to feel that 'harm' equals 'guilt', and ought to equal 'retribution', and a sense of frustration arises if it is found that this equation does not work out. This frustration at least partly underlies the demands for sterner penal measures, the reintroduction of corporal punishment and less attention to psychologists which are made from time to time by everyone from judges to speakers in women's meetings. While appreciating the unhappiness of those who find that the world is a very complex place and who long for sterner simplicities, we must continue to insist that 'consequences' and 'responsibility' are two quite different things.

The Social Sciences

Very roughly, we can divide the studies of man's behaviour into three fields: (1) that which concerns his behaviour in society, (2) that which concerns the way his body works, and (3) that which concerns the way his mind works. The dividing lines are not really as clear as this and work in one field often has implications for work in other fields – for example, the work on animal behaviour which is discussed below under the heading of the biological sciences is presented in an article written by a sociologist – but the headings will suffice for our very brief review.

The studies of man's behaviour in society, the social sciences, include sociology, economics, politics and education. They deal not only with the way man works through institutions, but also with the way in which institutions work upon man and limit his ability to act. The effects of social pressures on individual responsibility are seen most clearly when we consider extreme situations such as family failure and juvenile delinquency, but what we learn from studying society at the point where relationships break down is likely to give us some idea also of what is happening when relationships are what we would call normal.

In an article in *New Society* on 'An Approach to Delinquency', Bryan Wilson, Reader in Sociology at Oxford University, emphasized the converging effects of a number of changes that have been taking place in our society which tend to produce social disruption and delinquent behaviour. The first of these factors is the decline of the small, close-knit community, which has weakened the main institution through which social relationships were formerly learned and controlled.

As society has become more mobile and impersonal, and as relationships are increasingly between 'anonymous' people, so the influence of socialisation is less effectively reinforced by the agencies of social control – particularly outside work. Thus there occurs a breakdown of the wider social context of support for socialised behaviour. The burden of making the child a responsible citizen and inculcating those values which are meant to become part of the individual's 'mental set' towards the world falls increasingly on parents, rather than on more extensive social groups.[2]

Other factors include increased mobility, both physical and social, which has contributed to the weakening of the local community: for example, the school may no longer be a part of the place in which the children live, and the increased mobility of the teachers can weaken loyalties and reduce the sense of being a caring community within the school itself. A society which emphasizes achievement increases the frustrations of those who for various reasons are unable to 'get on':

Youthful violence and vandalism, and the inconvenience of the general public, provide young delinquents both with relief from frustration, and the occasion for stabbing back at the society which has frustrated them. The whole syndrome is supported by the approval which prevails for behaviour of this kind within the adolescent sub-culture, which defines the traditional moral values of society as 'phoney' and as something to be kicked against.[3]

Wilson notes also the substantial redistribution of income to 'younger people, and particularly to unskilled workers', and the influence of mass media which 'has as yet scarcely been assessed'.

The precise interplay of the factors Wilson mentions and their connection with ideas on delinquency put forward in other fields are matters for research and for argument: but at least we can say that they are influences which have to be taken into account before we can make any pronouncement about 'delinquency'. Our decisions to act can be very closely circumscribed by social factors, and moral responsibility is not a purely personal matter, but is bound up with our feelings towards society. How far is it reasonable to try to conform to the moral standards accepted by society, if the opportunities society offers consist of the worst housing, the worst schooling, and the least well-regarded and least well-paid work? In a study by Family Service Units of 129 families which formed their main load of long-term cases in 1954 it was found that

Nearly one third of these F.S.U. families were overcrowded according to the stringent standards of the 1936 Housing Act. This was considerably more than the national average and almost certainly higher than for working-class

[2] Bryan Wilson, 'An Approach to Delinquency,' *New Society*, 3 February, 1966, pp. 8–12.
[3] *Ibid.*

households generally. Moreover, by a standard which more realistically considered the needs of family life, over half the families had insufficient living space.[4]

This is an indication of one social factor among many which contribute to family breakdown. The relative importance of the various factors probably differs from person to person, and there is no possibility at present of drawing up a general theory of environmental influences and their relation to other influences.

Every social setting has its own moral conventions: there are some in which almost every child sooner or later acquires a police record; there are others in which tax-fiddles, adultery and a high consumption of spirits may be equally conventional. The capacity of the individual to make 'right' moral choices cannot be considered entirely apart from his social conditions; and if this is true, it implies a limitation on personal responsibility, for the influences which help to explain delinquent behaviour must also help to explain normal behaviour, so that even when we are 'good' we cannot necessarily take the credit.

The Biological Sciences

The studies which deal with man's physical functioning cover a narrower front than the social sciences, but the results are equally important. One example of information currently available from physiological studies is to be found in an article by D. H. Stott, Lecturer in Psychology at the University of Glasgow, which points out that in a study of thirty-three children in Glasgow who were classed as 'troublesome' the one common factor was not stressful family relationships (although nearly half did experience such relationships):

The most striking finding, applying to all the groups of troublesome children studied, was the large number of nervous and physical troubles with which they were afflicted – squints, speech defects, epilepsy, bed-wetting, poor muscular coordination, slight spastic tendencies, restless sleep, nervous mannerisms, chronic minor illnesses. In other words, they showed a strong tendency to multiple impairment, most of which was undoubtedly congenital in origin. It was therefore likely that they had also suffered damage to those parts of the nervous system which are the basis of behaviour.

The type of nervous damage from which they suffered seemed to make them susceptible to stresses which do not worry nervously tough children.

[4] A. F. Philp, *Family Failure* (London: Faber & Faber, 1963), p. 63.

They were in effect suffering from what we may describe as emotional handi-cap. This takes the form of a vulnerability, or a liability to resort to disturbed behaviour under stress or provocation. In a stable family a child who is only moderately affected will appear no doubt as sensitive, overemotional, very lacking in confidence, or lazy; but in a family wracked with quarrelling, threats of the mother to desert and other stresses, these vulnerable children go to pieces and become maladjusted and/or delinquent. . . . With the great advances that medical science has made since the Second World War, especially in the field of antibiotics, many more physically delicate children survive than previously. Among these will be a higher proportion of emotionally handi-capped than among the physically robust. Consequently we have a much larger reserve of vulnerable children, many of whom will become maladjusted and delinquent. With the attention now being given to saving children who would otherwise die at or soon after birth this tendency will be accentuated.[5]

Stott concludes that we need long-term measures to improve the conditons of pregnancy and childbirth, and short-term measures to detect and help the vulnerable children at an early age, including guidance for parents and for teachers 'in recognizing behaviour disturbance and dealing with it sympathetically rather than by punish-ment'.

The study of the genetical transmission of information and of the chemical basis of memory are also two fast-developing fields of research, but it is too early yet to say what conclusions may eventually be drawn about their relationship to behaviour patterns (*see Biology and Personality*, Oxford: Blackwell, 1965, a report of a symposium held in 1962, edited by Ian Ramsey).

The study of animal behaviour is beginning to have interesting implications for the study of human behaviour, particularly in relation to the effects of overcrowding. W. M. S. Russell, a sociologist at the University of Reading, surveys the field as follows:

The pioneer observations on monkey societies were made in zoos over 30 years ago by Sir Solly Zuckerman. They appeared to support the pessi-mistic view. These baboon societies were ruled by dictators, constantly bullying their subjects and taking a dictator's share of food. Quarrels were so frequent that such stern government was apparently essential, but nevertheless the societies frequently collapsed into indiscriminate violence.

But how do the beasts of the jungle behave *in* the jungle? Field studies of monkey and ape societies were more difficult, and they only became frequent after the Second World War. Each observer in turn reported with surprise

[5] D. H. Stott, 'Why Maladjustment?' *New Society*, 10 December, 1964, pp. 14–16.

that in his or her monkey species, obviously exceptional, societies in their natural surroundings were remarkably peaceful and free of tension, and serious fighting very rare. Eventually it was established that fighting is 'exceptionally' rare or absent in wild societies of gibbons, howler monkeys, African redtail monkeys, langurs, Japanese monkeys, gorillas, rhesus monkeys, bonnet macaque monkeys, chimpanzees, and several kinds of baboons, including the one studied by Zuckerman in the zoo. In a report published last summer, for instance, Vernon and Frances Reynolds describe the wild chimpanzees of the Budongo Forest in Uganda. During 300 hours of observation, they saw '17 quarrels involving actual fighting or displays of threat or anger', none lasting more than a few seconds. Evidently all the monkeys and apes are aggressive only when they are crowded together in a zoo.[6]

Russell also states that it has now been found with a great variety of higher animals that they show serious fighting only when they run short of space, and suggests that there may be a direct relation between a high population density and a high crime rate, and in particular one of the most distressing of all crimes – attacks by parents on children:

One special symptom of crowding, observed in monkeys, musk-rats, voles and Calhoun's rats, is the tendency to attack and even kill their own young. In 1961, 71 hospitals surveyed in the U.S.A. reported a total of 302 cases of children severely injured by their parents. Thirty three of the children died, and 85 suffered permanent brain injury. In 1957–64, of 764 people indicted in England for murder, 93 were accused of killing one or more of their own children (this is not counting cases where the victims were over 15 years of age).[7]

Studies of monkeys also show stress being passed on for several generations by disturbances of the behaviour of parents to their young: the American study showed that many of the parents ill-treating their children had themselves experienced similar behaviour from their own parents. Russell concludes by commenting on the value of communication in avoiding acts of violence in monkey societies, and the way in which human beings are separated not only by language barriers but even by 'manners, postures and facial expressions'; he points out that these barriers are much more serious among adults than they are among young children.

Psychology

Of the various schools of psychology, those concerned with psycho-

[6] W. M. C. Russell, 'Aggression: New Light from Animals,' *New Society*, 10 February, 1966, pp. 12–14.   [7] *Ibid.*

analysis are of most interest to the student of morals. Psychoanalysis, originating in the work of Freud, Jung and Adler, is concerned with the conscious and unconscious elements of the mind, and with our mental reactions to events, often going back into earliest childhood. Ranged against the theories of psychoanalysis, as an alternative to them and sometimes in direct opposition to them, are theories concerned with the physical origins of mental illness, and with physical methods of treatment, such as drugs and electric shock treatment.[8] There is a tendency for analysts to say that those who concentrate on physical methods run the risk of curing the symptoms rather than the causes of mental illness; to which the latter tend to reply that psychoanalysis is at best mere speculation: Sargent, later in the article quoted above (p. 33) writes of 'the much more speculative and uncertain types of psychiatric treatment theory propounded by Freud or even by Eysenck'. As usual in such disputes, the truth probably lies on both sides: undoubtedly some mental illnesses have physical origins, and some symptoms can be relieved by physical treatments; but equally certainly there is too solid a body of knowledge built up by the methods of psychoanalysis for it to be dismissed out of hand. For both approaches, what is known is less than what remains unknown: even Sargent claims to be able to cure only those who were already of 'good personality' before their illness.

Mental illness which has a physical origin and which responds to physical treatment can impair responsibility: a person's character may change after a serious accident involving damage to the brain; it can change also under the influence of drugs. Here it is the business of the psychiatrist rather than the moralist to attempt to assess what change has taken place, and why. The fact that physical conditions can affect the exercise of responsibility does not raise any fundamental moral problem: it neither proves nor disproves ideas about the existence and nature of 'personality'. This aspect of psychology we may therefore leave without further comment, and turn our attention to questions of psychoanalysis.

Alasdair MacIntyre, examining the claims of the psychoanalysts in *Encounter* ('The Psychoanalysts,' May 1965), concludes that psychoanalysis is more a faith than a science. The main problems are that

[8] Two further definitions may be useful: A 'psychiatrist' is someone who has received a general medical training and then specialized in the treatment of mental troubles, covering both those which are physical in origin and those which are not. A 'psychologist' is someone who has followed a course of study in psychology, but has not had a medical training.

psychoanalysis cannot show a significantly higher proportion of 'cures' than any other recognized method of psychiatric treatment; that it is difficult to distinguish between a 'cure' and a 'spontaneous remission' of a mental trouble; and that it is very difficult to say what we mean by a 'cure', in the sense that we cannot easily define what is a 'normal' state of mental health. We have, therefore, no way of checking the statements of psychoanalytic theory: there are symptoms, and there are theories about what causes them, but there is not as yet any necessary connection between the two. Dr John Wisdom, Reader in Logic and Scientific Method at the London School of Economics, summing up at a conference of the Society for Psychosomatic Research in 1958, commented on one of the papers:

Again it is the sort of thing that someone with clinical experience can hardly doubt, but there is a difference between having experiences on the basis of which you can hardly doubt something and providing proof. Proof is often unnecessary, but for certain purposes it is necessary – if you want to convince sceptical colleagues, or if there is reason to think a hypothesis may need refinement.[9]

He spoke also of occasions when 'intuitive, ordinary response to experience is enough to settle it without great bundles of statistics' (p. 262). This is the sort of ground on which much of psychoanalytic theory may be said to stand today, and it is a situation which is not altogether uncommon even in the experimental sciences (*see* the quotations from Professor W. T. Williams above, pp. 18f.); there are many areas of disagreement, and many conflicting claims, but there is also much common ground between the various schools of psychoanalytic thought. There is a certain amount of common ground also between psychoanalytic theory and theology (apart from the specifically religious ideas of such theorists as Jung).

The statements which psychoanalysis makes about our responsibility for our actions, put in a very simple form, are: (1) that much of our reaction to people and to events takes place in our unconscious minds, over which we do not have direct control; (2) that the mechanisms by which we deal with mental events are complex and devious, so that our outward actions may be expressing needs which have no apparent relationship to the direct objects of our actions, and of which we ourselves may be entirely unconscious; and (3) that the events which, unknown to us, may be motivating our present actions can

[9] *The Nature of Stress Disorder* (London: Hutchinson Medical Publications, 1959), p. 259.

sometimes have taken place a long way back in our lives – even in very early childhood. If we accept these statements, moral judgement both of others and of ourselves becomes much more difficult, because we have to look for hidden motives as well as overt ones; and although we have always looked for underlying motives in people's actions, psychoanalytic theory makes us look much deeper, and also tells us that this search is a matter for the professional, and that it can be dangerous in the hands of amateurs. It is, nevertheless, necessary that we should become amateurs in psychology, in order that we may at least pay sufficient attention to what psychologists say.

Let us take an example. In the summer of 1964 a national newspaper reported a case in which a boy came before a juvenile court for stealing a bicycle and £6. He was already on probation for an earlier offence, and it was said that the way he had been treated at school as a result of this first offence had made him decide to run away from home, in pursuit of which plan he had stolen the bicycle and the money. A medical report described the boy as 'a chronic nail-biter; neurotic and emotionally disturbed'. The court sent him to a detention centre for three months.[10] If we take the medical report seriously, the boy appears to be someone who in his life so far has not been given sufficient stability, security and affection. His offences could therefore be seen to be in the nature of a cry for help: a combination of an emotional safety valve to relieve pressures which are felt to be intolerable, and an appeal to society at large to take some action and to show some understanding. The decision of the magistrates had the effect of taking this boy in his condition of emotional damage and placing him for the next three months in a situation carefully designed to provide a special degree of emotional tension and hostile oversight. Whatever the weaknesses of psychoanalytic theory, even a little attention to it (or even to the Christian idea of love) might have saved the magistrates – and all of us, in our various decisions – from a mistake like this.

Our capacity for making moral judgements is to some extent governed by our own psychological history. For example, if we react violently against certain sorts of behaviour, this can be a defence against an unconscious attraction to the same behaviour; if we strenuously advocate corporal punishment, this may be a way of letting our own sadistic (or masochistic) impulses have some exercise. Each of us has in his own unconscious some of the desires and attrac-

[10] *Daily Herald*, 15 July, 1964.

tions he deplores in other people. Freda Fordham, explaining the Jungian concept of 'the shadow', writes: 'The shadow is the personal unconscious; it is all those uncivilised desires and emotions that are incompatible with social standards and our ideal personality, all that we are ashamed of, all that we do not want to know about ourselves. It follows that the narrower and more restrictive the society in which we live the larger will be our shadow.'[11]

Limited Responsibility

How far can we speak of 'responsibility' in the face of the results of such studies as these in the fields of sociology, biology and psychology? The results of the various studies do not as yet present us with a coherent and assured account of human behaviour; but they produce some explanations of behaviour, and these explanations tend to reduce the scope of our responsibility. They show that there are restraints upon our freedom to act, and that there are pressures which tend to make us act in certain ways. The important word, however, is *tend*.

Even studies in psychology, which have the most to say about human motivation, do not rule out moral choice: the ability of psychology to account for human behaviour after the event does not make our choices entirely predictable before the event. Treatment which makes one human being repressed, docile and depressive may make another rebellious, angry and even creative. The differences in response to various psychological situations between one person and another may be ascribed to differences of heredity and of environment, but they may be ascribed also, at least partly, to free moral choice.

The situation therefore is that science can say, 'You are doing this because you have a certain genetical make-up, a certain psychological make-up, and a certain set of environmental influences'; but that we can still reply, 'I do this also because I choose to do it'. The fact that we feel free to act, and feel responsible for our actions – the fact that we use moral language at all – is evidence in favour of the existence of moral choice. What we cannot do (and are not likely ever to be able to do) is to divide the behaviour of other people into various strands and say, 'He was 37% responsible for his actions at this point'. Even for our own actions we have only a partial idea of how far we act from choice.

[11] Freda Fordham, *An Introduction to Jung's Psychology* (London: Penguin Books, 1961), p. 50.

The Christian Idea of Responsibility

The Christian idea of responsibility may be defined in two statements: that we are responsible for our actions, and that we do not judge others.

We are responsible for our actions in the dynamic sense that we can overcome both the external pressures of society and environment and the internal pressures of genetics and psychology and begin to act, by the power of God in us, as people who have nothing to fear and nothing to lose. It is not a question of finding a chink for personal responsibility between the findings of sociology, biology and psychology, but of learning, by power given and received, to take control of what we are. Responsibility, therefore, is not so much concerned with what we have done in the past, nor even with doing good acts now – because that is not yet entirely within our control – but with growing in grace, without which good acts are not possible.

In saying this we do not underrate the difficulties. The idea of the 'unconscious' ought to have caused little surprise to theologians; Paul was well aware of the existence of inner compulsions and in his letter to the Romans he says:

I do not even acknowledge my own actions as mine, for what I do is not what I want to do, but what I detest. But if what I want to do is against my will, it means I agree with the law and hold it to be admirable. But as things are, it is no longer I who perform the action, but sin that lodges in me. For I know that nothing good lodges in me – in my unspiritual nature, I mean – for though the will to do good is there, the deed is not. The good which I want to do, I fail to do; but what I do is the wrong which is against my will; and if what I do is against my will, clearly it is no longer I who am the agent, but sin that has its lodging in me (7.15–20).

Compare this with the Freudians' phrase: 'We are lived by our unconscious' (Groddeck, quoted in J. A. C. Brown, *Freud and the Post-Freudians*, London: Penguin, 1961, p. 10). But Paul goes on to ask 'who is there to rescue me out of this body doomed to death?' and answers 'God alone, through Jesus Christ our Lord' (vv. 24–5). Christian experience holds that we can, some easily and some with difficulty, cease to be lived by our unconscious and by any other pressure, by consciously living in God, and that we stand to be judged not so much by the amount of good or of harm that we do as by the seriousness of our desire to try for the good.

When we turn to consider our attitude to other people's actions, we are concerned with needs rather than with judgement. It is not so much our business to see how far others are responsible for their actions as to see how far we can help them. In fact we still have to attempt to assess responsibility, because until we know how far a person is acting deliberately, and how far under some pressure, we do not know fully what his or her needs are. The important distinction to be made is that this assessment is not to be used for purposes of judgement – 'this is a bad person', 'this is a good person' – but simply so that we may know what we can do for them.

If people are being awkward and are behaving in a manner which we consider reprehensible, the only effective action we can take is to try to understand them and to help them. Anselm, who became Archbishop of Canterbury in 1093, answered complaints from those who had to deal with the unruly children in the abbey school by recommending 'sympathy, patience and affection' (Dom David Knowles, *Saints and Scholars*), and the same advice applies to our dealings with adults. It is difficult to have enough confidence in our fellow men to believe that this approach will work (and it has not always been believed by the Church itself), but it has always been the foundation of Christian teaching about human relationships and it is the only foundation for any sane approach to our fellow human beings by anyone of any belief.

There are, of course, many sayings in the New Testament about judgement and punishment, but these are not about human judgement; rather they refer to the possibility of rejecting God knowingly (the 'sin against the Holy Spirit') and, however picturesque their form, are essentially statements about the moral nature of the universe and the inevitable effects of choosing to turn away from love.

Julian of Norwich, writing in the second half of the fourteenth century, describes a vision in which she sees mankind as a servant, going to do the will of Christ:

> The Servant, not only he goeth, but suddenly he starteth, and runneth in great haste, for to do his Lord's will. And anon he falleth into a slade (*sc. a steep hollow place*) and taketh full great hurt . . . I marvelled how this Servant might meekly suffer there all this woe, and I beheld with carefulness to learn if I could perceive in him any fault, or if the Lord should assign to him any blame. And in sooth there was none seen: for only his goodwill and his great desire was cause of his falling.[12]

[12] Julian of Norwich, *Revelation of Divine Love* (London: Methuen, 1927), chap. 51.

She explains the figure of the Servant as follows:

> The Servant that stood afore the Lord, I understood that it was shewed for Adam: that is to say, one man was shewed, that time, and his falling, to make it thereby understood how God beholdeth All-Man and his falling. For in the sight of God all man is one man, and one man is all man.[13]

The implications of this understanding of the nature of all men for our daily treatment of one another find a more conventional voice in John Tauler, Friar-Preacher of Strasburg in the Middle Ages:

> For when we see men punishing and oppressing with such vehemence those who are under them, or treating them so harshly, with sharp words and sour looks, it is to be feared that there is more reproof given out of crabbed impatience than for the sake of charity and kindness, especially by those who have not yet experienced the inward joy of hearty sweetness and godly love; for the soul that has not yet experienced inward love and divine sweetness, does yet know how to hold a discreet mien and just language in rebuking; but genuine love teaches us how we ought to treat those who are worthy of punishment.
>
> Now, let him who has to punish, in virtue of his office, first take account of God's dishonour and the injury done to the souls of his flock; and then rebuke with sweet, loving words, and patient demeanour and gestures; so that the weak shall be able to mark that he is seeking and purposing their welfare alone and nothing else.[14]

We may note that Tauler uses the word 'punishment'. By this he seems to mean more 'reform' – a way of setting the weak on the right path again – than 'retribution'; but he does take account of the amount of harm that has been done. It is important that understanding should not be confused with weakness. Children need firmness within a context of love and adults also need, in some circumstances, a response which brings them up short, and challenges them to see what they are doing. But anyone who sets out to administer such a rebuke needs to be very certain that it is to be done because it meets the real need of the other person, and not because we feel like giving it: and this is possible only if it is done within a genuine compassion for and understanding of the other – and only if we ourselves are, as Tauler again says, secure in the inward experience of the sweetness and power of God.

There are also times when sympathy, patience and affection fail, either because of our ignorance (there are psychological conditions

[13] *Ibid.*

[14] John Tauler, *The Inner Way* (London: Methuen, 1903), Sermon 12.

which we do not yet know how to help), or because there is no response from the other; and then we have to find other methods – but when we do, at least we should not congratulate ourselves upon them.

Wholeness and Freedom

Neither psychology nor the biological sciences nor sociology can give an adequate definition of what we mean by a 'normal' person, or provide a universally acceptable set of social and individual goals. Sargent, in the article already quoted (above, pp. 33, 41), says in his penultimate paragraph: 'We shall also see an end to the need for all elaborate psychotherapy, and even spiritual help, which has until recently been thought to be so necessary for a cure.' But he also says in his final paragraph:

Once we have the brain functioning normally again, it is then that the priest and politician should come along, take over the reins, and tell us all what we should be doing with our renewed courage, happiness in living and our restored and fully functioning mental talents.

What he does not say is how he comes by his particular definition of normal functioning (whatever it may be), nor, for that matter, what he means by the phrase quoted earlier, 'previously good personality'. Barbara Wootton, in *Social Science and Social Pathology*, has a severe analysis of various attempts to define 'mental health' (Part II, chapters 7 to 9), all of which are either circular, or too vague to be of any use, or attempts to elevate into sociological principles the writer's own particular beliefs.

The fact is that we cannot define terms like 'mental health', or 'normal personality', or 'happiness', without recourse to some assumptions about the nature of man and of the world we live in; and try as we may we cannot logically give such assumptions any status other than that of 'beliefs'. The Christian belief about 'normal' mental health is that it is not primarily a state of integration with oneself, or with society, but with God. God can be met in other people, in the physical universe and directly; and by all these ways growth in the knowledge of God at work leads to a greater understanding of and ability to relate to other people, and to a growing understanding of and ability to live with oneself (for which the technical theological words are charity, grace, humility and peace).

Christian dependence on God sometimes seems, to those who are not committed to religious belief, to deny the dignity of man as a free being, and therefore to be offensive. No amount of argument can remove this sense of offence, because the real difficulty is the existence of God himself; but at least the question of belief should not be confused with the question of freedom. There is a neutral sense of the word 'free' by which we mean that we have a number of choices, all of which are of roughly equal value and interest to us: this may be true, for example, when we buy soup or choose a holiday resort. But this is not what we mean when we are talking of political or moral freedom: here 'freedom' means that we are not prevented forcibly from doing something which we very much want to do, such as criticizing the government in public or practising our religion. We are not worried if there is not an alternative choice which would be equally attractive to us – if we achieve civil liberty we do not feel 'unfree' because we have not the option of being locked up for our opinions. The Christian finds that in committing himself to God he is freer than ever before, because for the first time he begins to discover who he is and what he wants. Our freedom is increased because new possibilities of being open up to us and also because it becomes possible to overcome finally the pressures which bind us both from without and from within.

The Christian dependence on God is a little like falling in love; and like the marriage which follows falling in love it has its own difficulties, adjustments and disappointments, and its own dull patches; but like marriage, it sets limits on our freedom only as a necessary preliminary to the deeper exploration and adventure which is the nature of commitment, either to God or to another person. It is the exploration and the adventure that we are really talking about when we use the words 'freedom' and 'responsibility'.

PART TWO

PRACTICAL APPLICATIONS

4

THE CRIMINAL LAW

THE criminal offender is often someone who is in greater need of help emotionally and spiritually than the person he has offended. People do not on the whole enter upon a life of crime after a process of rational consideration, and many criminals are among the people who are least able to foresee consequences and act upon them. However unpalatable the fact may be, what little we do know about criminals suggests that they are people who *need* help (repeat, 'need', not 'want') rather than punishment. A man's 'guilt' depends not only on what he has done, but also on *why* he has done it and some of the most revolting actions are done by the most pathetic people. Once this fact is realized, the whole basis of the criminal law is laid open to question and doubts which are raised by the study of psychology reinforce those which are raised by the study of moral theology about the concepts of 'punishment' and of 'responsibility'.

Responsibility

When John Doe[1] stands in the dock accused of a crime, the Court first of all wants to know 'the facts'. Was he really in Gas Alley on the night of the twenty-fourth of November, did he climb over a fence into the back yard of Messrs Smith and Jones, and did he then force open the office window and climb into the building? All this may be fairly easy to establish. Included among the facts, however, are John Doe's own knowledge and intentions. We have already seen that human action is a very complex matter. John Doe, who stole in Gas Alley on the night of the twenty-fourth, is one particular man, whose father was a particular sort of person, who grew up in a particular area,

[1] 'John Doe' is a fictitious name often used for hypothetical legal cases. 'Gas Alley' and 'Smith and Jones' are also fictitious names.

went to a particular school, made a particular set of friends, was
introduced to a particular set of moral ideas under conditions which
may or may not have been favourable to their acceptance, and on top
of all this has made his own particular moral choices, may or may not
have a wife and family, and may or may not be out of a job. All this
has to be included in the facts of what John Doe did, and if the Court is
to assess his responsibility it needs to take account of all these factors –
but can it do so? The answer, briefly, is 'No'.

A full assessment of responsibility is not within the ability of a
Court, or of any human being. Even a rough assessment is extremely
difficult. Where 'diminished responsibility' is allowed as a defence,
it is a matter notoriously difficult to define. Writing of the connection
between mental disorder and responsibility, Professor H. L. A. Hart
says: 'Proof of mental elements – especially to juries – is a difficult
matter, and the law has often abandoned the attempt to discover
whether a person charged with a crime actually intended to do it . . .'[2]
In fact the Courts find it very difficult to assess responsibility at all.
They can probably establish enough about the offender and the offence
to have some idea of what sort of treatment might be of help to him,
or what sort of restraint is necessary for his own protection and the
protection of other people, and in establishing these matters they will
have regard to what they can discover about his intentions, his ability
to distinguish 'right' and 'wrong', and his ability to foresee and to
act upon the foresight of the possible consequences of his action. They
will try to decide whether any of the results of his action could be
called accidental, and whether there were circumstances of which he
was ignorant, and if so, whether he could and should have made
himself better informed – but all this falls well short of an accurate
assessment of 'responsibility', and of moral 'guilt', because there are
too many things that we do not know for certain.

Law and Morals

The next thing the Court wants to know is whether what John Doe
did is against the law. The law, like the facts, is fairly easy to settle
as an immediate practical question, but behind it there lie important
questions of principle about the existence of the law itself and about

[2] H. L. A. Hart, *Punishment and the Elimination of Responsibility* (London: The
Athlone Press, 1962), p. 21.

when it should or should not intervene. Why has the Court got John Doe in the dock for this particular act and whose interests is it trying to protect? The short answers to these two questions are 'Because John Doe has done something wrong', and 'The Court is trying to protect the rest of us'; but both these statements need considerable qualification.

John Doe stands in the dock because breaking and entering, and stealing, are wrong. Fornication is also thought by many people to be wrong, but nobody stands in the dock of a Criminal Court for it, so long as it is done in private. At some point it has been decided that the law should take notice of the one, but not of the other. This is only one example out of many differences that exist between the law and the normal moral code of people who still have some attachment to Christianity. The relation of the law to morals is complex and ambiguous: in one sense the law supports morals, and in another sense it does not.

The law supports, and is supported by, morals because what it forbids is derived from what the moral code forbids (though there is now quite a large field of regulatory legislation which has no direct connection with moral attitudes). From the earliest times the law in the western world has been derived from a moral code, either from such notions as 'truth' and 'justice' as part of a 'natural law', or from the Christian faith. Men have understood that what makes things right or wrong is not that the law says so, but that the universe has a moral structure which the law attempts to reflect. This approach has kept the law free from arbitrariness: law has not been at the mercy of the mere ideas of a king or emperor or dictator, to be made one day and unmade the next; there has been stability and continuity in the law's attitude to each kind of action. Men have known from year to year and even from century to century what will be permitted and what will not, if, at any time, the law has become unjust, it has been open to someone to challenge it in the name of the moral code – in the name of 'justice', or of 'liberty' – and even if this has not always been a very realistic thing to do in the short run, in the long run such words have a power which is able to bring down unjust laws and the people who make them. Today we still need the same protection: unless the law is based upon morality we have no defence against the ruling body – and that can be disastrous whether we are dealing with a king or with a president or with a democratic parliament, for the will of the people can bear just as hard as the will of the crown. The only barrier against legislative injustice is that the law should be acknowledged, by those who make it, by those who administer it, and by the community at large, to derive from a fixed morality. It is this safeguard that Christian moral principles have provided for us through the law in modern times.

Law and Freedom

On the other hand, the law cannot deal with everything that the moral code holds to be wrong. This is a practical matter – we do not have the resources to pursue by law every breach of morals – but it is also a question of the way in which we define the relationship between the individual and society.

At one extreme is the argument that individual liberty is one of the highest values that society exists to promote, and that therefore the business of the law is to protect us from outside interference, but to leave our private lives alone. For example, if a man gets drunk in his own room, that is a private act, but if he staggers about the streets offending women and frightening children, that is a public act and becomes the concern of the law; if a man is a thief, that is public business, but if he is a miser, that is his own business. In the strictest sense of the words there are, of course, no such things as 'private acts', because every action has an effect not only on the doer but also on his relations with others: an alcoholic loses mental and physical efficiency and becomes less desirable as a father or as a motorist; even suicide is an act which impinges upon other people. Nevertheless, a commonsense and usable distinction exists between actions which harm others and actions which do not, and it is not beyond our power to observe it in the making of laws. In the words of John Stuart Mill: '. . . the sole end for which mankind are warranted, individually or collectively, in interfering with the liberty of action of any of their number, is self-protection.'[3] Like most famous definitions this could be made to mean many things, and the great difficulty is to define how far we are entitled to take action against someone for their own protection, but the general drift of Mill's argument is clear: that the presumption is always against taking action by law, that it needs a very strong argument and a demonstrable harm being done to justify forcible intervention, and that in any event we are not entitled to take action against someone for the protection of a mythical entity

[3] John Stuart Mill, *On Liberty*, chap. 1.

called 'society', conceived as something more than the sum of the separate interests of the individuals who compose it.

At the other extreme is the argument that the first business of society is to protect itself and to ensure its own continued existence, and that any steps taken in pursuit of this aim may be legitimate, even though they could not be justified on the basis of the individual interests involved. Lord Devlin, commenting on the Report of the Committee on Homosexual Offences and Prostitution (the Wolfenden Report), says:

> The error of jurisprudence in the Wolfenden Report is caused by the search for some single principle to explain the division between sin and crime. The Report finds it in the principle that the criminal law exists for the protection of individuals; on this principle fornication in private between consenting adults is outside the law and thus it becomes logically indefensible to bring homosexuality between consenting adults in private within it. But the true principle is that the law exists for the protection of society.[4]

This is saying either too little or too much: too little if we are left with the impression that the sole aim of the law is the protection of society as it is, without regard to the quality of that society (some societies do not deserve to survive); too much if we are left with the impression that the rights of society – except very rarely, in the moments of greatest danger (and even this is arguable) – are greater than the rights of the individual in it. We may accept what Lord Devlin says to this extent, that the good of one man cannot be separated from the good of all men and that we should be in a poor way if society folded up; but we should be in an even worse way if we elevated the protection of society as the highest aim of the law. The highest aim of the law is the protection of the individual. To say otherwise is to misunderstand the whole basis of morals, for the primary principle of moral action is that it is free action – and this necessarily implies some freedom to make and to carry out wrong moral choices. The one uniquely valuable thing in the world is an individual human being, and whether or not society is worth preserving

---

[4] Sir Patrick Devlin, *The Enforcement of Morals* (London: Oxford University Press, 1959), p. 1. This view received the support of the House of Lords in Shaw v. D.P.P. (1961) 2 W.L.R. 917 ('The Ladies' Directory' case): Viscount Simonds said: 'In the sphere of criminal law I entertain no doubt that there remains in the courts of law a residual power to enforce the supreme and fundamental purpose of law, to conserve not only the safety and order but also the moral welfare of the state, and that is is their duty to guard it against attacks which may be the more insidious because they are novel and unprepared for.'

depends precisely on how far it recognizes this value even in those who do not conform to its morals.

The Authority of the Law

When the law-making body decides whether to act or not to act, it does so in a manner which is peculiar to itself.

Law-making is a complex process: the sovereign power has to consider not only the basic principle of what the law is for, and the moral code which the law attempts to express, but also the facts of the society in which it is operating. Law enforcement is possible only if the general public is willing to keep the law, if the police have confidence in their job, if juries are willing to convict and magistrates are willing to give more than nominal sentences, and laws will not be passed at all unless the legislators are sure of substantial political or military support. Consequently there are some matters about which it might be morally right to pass a law, but socially and economically impossible: the law of Rome, in a society which was entirely committed to the institution of slavery, economically, politically and philosophically, could not have produced, much less enforced, Lord Mansfield's dictum, 'Let the black go free'. Today the public in Britain is made up of everybody from a Hindu immigrant to a member of the Exclusive Bretheren, and the business of the law-making body is to reconcile the interests of all of us. Consequently the resulting law is unlikely to conform exactly to any one moral code.

When all has been said, John Doe stands in the dock because Parliament has said that anyone who commits this particular sort of action shall stand in the dock for it. It is important to remember this when we talk about 'criminals', because it is easy to fall into the way of thinking that the law really does 'uphold morals' quite simply, and that therefore anyone who is a criminal at law must be an immoral person. The truth about John Doe is that he is in the dock because we have decided to put him there, and the question of his morality or immorality is an entirely different matter.

Retribution

When the facts of a case have been established, and when it is clear that what was done is illegal, we come to the sentence, and to the question of what we are going to do about John Doe. At this point the Court may have three things in mind: (1) a desire to punish John Doe, (2) a desire to deter him and others from future offences, and (3) a desire to help him to become a better man. Of these elements of a judicial sentence, the main emphasis until recent times has been upon retribution, and a purely retributive element is still claimed for the action of the law. In his evidence to *The Royal Commission on Capital Punishment*, Lord Denning says:

... the punishment for grave crimes should adequately reflect the revulsion felt by the great majority of citizens for them. It is a mistake to consider the object of punishment as being deterrent or reformative or preventive and nothing else. The ultimate justification of any punishment is not that it is a deterrent but that it is the emphatic denunciation by the community of the crime . . .[5]

It is true that there is an element of denunciation in the processes of law and that the law is a moral educator in the sense that the community by the trial, verdict and sentence (if any) declares that the act in question is not (or is) acceptable: Hugh J. Klare points out that the one experience that all the first offenders who do not offend again have in common is the trial and verdict (*Anatomy of Prison*, London: Penguin, 1962, p. 26). Stopping a man from repeating an offence is not, of course, the same as leading him to see that the action was wrong, and it is not clear how far anyone can be converted to a positive belief by 'denunciation'; for some people a public rebuke may act as a trigger for a change already building up in them, but conversion of any sort is not a necessary result of conviction and sentence, either for the offender or for anyone following the case.

But the difficulty about Lord Denning's view is that 'emphatic denunciation' does not stop at a verbal rebuke: we tend to go on to a sentence that puts a man in prison for six months or fines him twenty pounds. Where such a penalty is awarded for the sake of 'emphatic denunciation', or for the 'vindication' of the law – that is, where it is seeking to make a moral point, rather than to deter or to reform – we are, in effect, returning evil for evil; we are trying to inflict on the offender some harm which is commensurate with the harm that he himself has done. Such a retributive or vindicative idea of the law raises a practical objection and a moral objection.

The practical objection is that, as we have already seen, it is difficult, if not impossible, for a Court to assess 'responsibility' with any

[5] *The Royal Commission on Capital Punishment*, Report (London: H.M.S.O., 1953), para. 53.

semblance of accuracy. If we cannot say how far a man is responsible, we cannot say how far he should be punished. The process is so crude as to cast doubts on its value, even without the moral objection; nevertheless we have to continue to attempt to assess responsibility to protect the offender, even if not to punish him (*see below*, 'Protecting the Offender' pp. 65–67).

The moral objection is that on Christian terms the power to punish does not exist: moral judgement in this sense is reserved to God and resides neither in the individual nor in the community. Even if this extreme position is not accepted (and it is possible to argue the other way), it remains true that so far from conveying moral information retribution conveys only immoral information, namely, that violence works in stronger hands. The deliberate infliction of pain and suffering as a moral act can show only that we believe in pain and suffering as moral means. The report of the Church of England committee which studied the subject, issued in 1963, cautiously hints at this objection when it says: '. . . it is not easy to specify activities which *both* register moral disapproval *and also* conform to, say, the "charity" which "beareth and endureth all things", a charity which of course must extend to the victim as much as to the offender.'[6]

An Example to Others

The idea of sentencing one man in such a way as to deter others from committing a similar offence also constitutes a grave moral problem.

'Exemplary' sentences are by no means unknown in our Courts, but they are morally very doubtful, insofar as they treat the offender more as an object-lesson than as a person, and thereby degrade him – and whatever reduces the value of one human reduces the value of all of us. The offender has the rights of a human being by virtue of existing, not by virtue of living up to a standard that someone else has set for him and after his offence he remains a human being. He must be dealt with for his offence, but we are not entitled to do anything, so to speak, 'extra' to him by way of general warning to other people.

It is sometimes argued that in committing an offence a man sets aside some of his own rights, so that to that extent we may use him

---

[6] *Punishment*, (London: Church Information Office, 1963), p. 32.

as a lesson to others, but this argument cannot be sustained, for three reasons. Firstly, it is difficult to see why this 'setting aside' should take place; secondly, to judge such a 'setting aside' of rights would be as difficult as judging 'responsibility' – in short, it would be impracticable; thirdly, to set aside a man's rights for the sake of the possible future wrongdoing of others arising from his example would be to punish him for a purely hypothetical consideration, which is hardly just.

When a man does wrong he is not any the less a human being: we, all of us, are wrong sometimes, and moral progress consists very largely in realizing more and more how wrong we ourselves can be. What human values are involved in 'exemplary' sentencing the reader may care to work out for himself or herself from the following example, reproduced in full from the Law Report in *The Guardian* (proper names have been omitted to prevent easy identification of those concerned):

Exemplary Sentences were 'Fully Justified'
Court of Criminal Appeal

R. V. J——
R. V. C——

Before the Lord Chief Justice (Lord Parker), Mr Justice Sachs, and Mr Justice Widgery.

The court dismissed the appeal of the appellant J—— and refused application of the appellant C—— for leave to appeal.

Both had pleaded guilty at E—— assizes before Mr Justice Megaw to a riotous assembly, assault occasioning actual bodily harm, common assault, and possessing an offensive weapon. Both were sentenced to Borstal training and J—— was appealing against that sentence by leave of a single judge. C—— was applying for leave to appeal against sentence, such leave having previously been refused by the single judge.

The appellants were charged with four other youths and all were convicted. Counsel had submitted in the case of J—— that the sentence was too severe in view of the fact that J—— had not been in serious trouble before and that since the incident he had married and was providing for his wife and illegitimate child; and that he had severed all connection with his old and undesirable friends.

Lamentable

Lord Parker, giving judgement, said that the present case disclosed a lamentable state of affairs in the D—— and L—— areas. On the night in question these two youths in their gang of 25, ran riot, assaulting people and property.

It all started when these youths in E—— were told that the D—— youths had come and attacked people and smashed up a public-house at W—— C——.

During the escapade two young men were attacked and struck down. One escaped, the other was kicked and punched while he was on the ground. Then at a coffee bar two other youths were attacked, though they said they were not from D——. They were kicked and knocked down, one received superficial lacerations, the other required five stitches. Both J—— and C—— made false statements and said that the purpose of the attack was to reap vengeance.

Lord Parker said that that behaviour was quite disgraceful and that if ever an exemplary sentence was called for it was in the present case. J—— was 19 and the Court had been told that he had given up the present kind of offence: he was married, and the probation officer felt that he had learnt his lesson, had become more responsible, and was taking seriously the fact that he had to support a wife and her illegitimate child. The Borstal Governor had taken the trouble to come to court and was satisfied that J—— had learnt his lesson and needed little training, only supervision.

C——, on the other hand, was 17, with a bad work record, and had been put on probation on the previous year for larceny and taking and driving away a motor vehicle. The Court was quite satisfied that an exemplary sentence was called for and in that it was thinking not so much of reform but of punishment. The Court was determined that the present sort of thing must stop and the only way to stop it was by sending people to prison or to Borstal. The appeal of J—— would be dismissed and C——'s application for leave to appeal would be refused.[7]

Bearing in mind the fact that, as this report shows, the criminal is often someone whose behaviour is genuinely unpleasant, we can put out of our minds any idea that all any criminal needs is 'a little kindness'; on the other hand, we can also put out of our minds the too-easy assumption of the Court that 'exemplary' sentences do deter: as the Home Office handbook for Courts on the treatment of offenders says: 'Very little is so far known about the deterrent effect on the population as a whole of sentences passed on particular offenders.'[8]

The questions then remain: (1) What good is done to J——, to his wife and to his child, by this 'exemplary' sentence? (2) What sort of society are we that we prefer to 'punish' J—— rather than to consider his likely future? (3) What sort of society are we that we punish J—— as much for what others have done in the past or may do in the future as for what he himself has done?

[7] *The Guardian*, 15 February, 1966.
[8] Home Office, *The Sentence of the Court* (London, H.M.S.O., 1964), p. 40, para. 152.

Deterring the Offender

How we prevent an offender from repeating his offence is, or ought to be, largely a question of fact. What are the causes of the offender's action? What methods of dealing with him are available? What is their relative effectiveness? The facts on the first question, as we have already seen, are complex; the facts on the second question are easy enough to find; the facts on the third question are only slowly beginning to emerge. The Home Office Research Unit is carrying out several studies of the effects of different sentences, one of which is of all offenders convicted in the Metropolitan Police District during March and April 1957; the main points which have emerged from this study are as follows:

(*a*) Fines were followed by the fewest reconvictions compared with the expected numbers for both first offenders and recidivists of almost all age groups.

(*b*) Probation produced relatively better results (in comparison with the calculated expectation) when used for offenders with previous convictions than when used for first offenders, although at best the results were only about equal to expectation.

(*c*) Approved school results were also better for offenders with previous offences. (The poor results for first offenders may be accounted for by poor home backgrounds, since it is exceptional for first offenders to be given this treatment.)

(*d*) Detention centre results tended to be slightly inferior to borstal results.

(*e*) Imprisonment results were better (compared with the expected results) for offenders with previous convictions than for first offenders, except among those aged 30 or over, but since the proportion of first offenders in this age-group who are reconvicted is, in any event, very small, too much reliance should not be placed on these figures.[9] (*The 'expected result' is an attempt by the research team to predict a normal rate of reconviction according to such variables as age, type of offence, and previous history.*)

On the whole, fines and discharges seem to be most effective treatment for most offenders, on the basis of reconviction rates, but the effectiveness varies according to age, to the type of offence and to the background of the offender. The variations in the sentencing policies of different Courts make genuine comparisons very difficult.

The large body of knowledge that already exists about human behaviour needs to be applied on a large scale, and with an adequate

9 *Ibid.*, p. 49, para. 161.

amount of money, to the treatment of the criminal offender. Only when this is done shall we be in a position to make firmer statements about deterrence. The Home Office already has under way a number of experiments of great interest, including group counselling for prisoners and prison staffs, new types of Borstal aftercare, and new types of prisons; similar work is in progress in other countries. The best way of deterring an offender is to get down to the causes of his action and see if they can be changed, and this is the line which penal theory and penal practice are beginning to take. One of the most impressive examples is the Borstal aftercare experiment known as 'Northways', which aims to provide something approaching a normal home, together with psychological support and interpretation, for boys who have hardly known a normal home life and who, on the basis of their past history, are highly likely to continue in a life of crime. The results of this experiment so far are encouraging (*see* Derek Miller, *Growth to Freedom*, London: Tavistock Publications, 1964). In advance of scientific decisions about the best way to treat offenders, it seems fairly safe to predict that we shall continue to move away from the concepts of 'punishment' and 'deterrence' towards the concept of treatment.

We are also likely to move towards putting more emphasis on discovering potential offenders in childhood, and helping them more effectively. A better application of what we already know about children with behavioural difficulties (by the use of more trained workers and more money both in the home and in the school) would probably bring about a considerable reduction in the crime rate. Thought on the treatment of juvenile offenders is tending to the idea of dealing with them as far as possible within the local community, even to the extent of providing hostels connected with the schools for those who need residential supervision, so that the child can maintain contact with the rest of his family and with the community. This sort of 'family service' may be expensive – but so is crime.

The idea of regarding the offender as someone who needs treatment rather than punishment – and of providing treatment through early detection and preventive measures – should be welcome both because it springs from a higher regard for human beings than does the demand for punishment and deterrence by fear, and also because it is likely to be more effective in preventing crime. It should not surprise us so much as it sometimes does that in a God-made world compassion and understanding really do work better than revulsion and fear; but at the same time it is worth repeating that 'understanding' means 'being realistic', and that 'compassion' does not exclude 'restraint'.

A substantial part of the answer to crime will always (or at least for the foreseeable future) lie in providing an effective police presence and a high rate of detection, whatever we do with the offender when we have him. At the time when we are turning to ideas of 'treatment' rather than 'punishment' a great deal of attention needs to be paid to the goals of police work and to the morale of the members of the police forces. It is the policeman more than anyone else who has to bear the tension between concern for the offender and concern for the victim and for the law, and this tension is likely to increase rather than decrease in the future. One major example is the fact that the laws of evidence are designed to prevent, so far as possible, any innocent person being found guilty in error: the consequence is that the police feel that they 'know' a great many things that they cannot prove in Court, and the resulting sense of frustration may be at least part of the explanation for the occasional examples of police violence and of falsification of evidence. If to our concern for the innocent man there is to be added a further concern for the welfare of the convicted offender, society will have to decide more clearly what it wants the police to be and to do and how far their work is to be judged by the rates of crimes committed and of offenders detected; and how far it is prepared to provide the means for the police to do their work effectively. It may be that the functions of detection and the enforcement of the law cannot be combined with an attempt to understand the fundamental motivation of the offender and a desire to help him as a person, but it is interesting that the first move towards such a combination of functions has originated within the police forces themselves in the preventive work being carried out among juveniles by several forces.

Protecting the Offender

The great danger in changing penal theory and practice from the idea of 'retribution' to the idea of 'treatment' is that we may find ourselves imposing greater penalties on the offender in the name of 'treatment' than he would have received in the name of 'punishment', because what may seem to us to be a move for his own good may appear to him to be simply a different sort of penalty. This difficulty already arises in our dealings with children whom we deem to be in need of 'care and protection'. When, for example, a child is taken

C

into the care of a local authority under a 'fit person' order, this can easily appear to the child and to the relatives, as a form of punishment; indeed, the phrase 'put away' is often used by people in this context. A child who has committed a series of small offences and who has inadequate parents can often be 'put away' for ten years or more, which is a severe sentence by any standards, however much our intention may be to help. The situation is made more difficult by the fact that an offender's 'needs' are not necessarily related to the 'seriousness' of his offence, so that no 'tariff of treatment' related to the old idea of a 'tariff of punishments' could be drawn up.

There is no way of prevening injustices altogether in a system which aims to help the offender any more than there is in a system which aims to punish the offender, but certain safeguards may be suggested.

The first, and most fundamental, is that it should be clear throughout the penal system that the first object in dealing with the offender is to respect him as a human being, and to try to help him. As in a punitive system the safeguard for the prisoner is the concept of 'justice', so it remains in a system that is not punitive, but with a marginal note that 'justice' is an aspect of 'love'. It is the ethos of a system, rather than its precise rules, which is the best guarantee of its right working – as we may see by the history of the attempts to transplant parliamentary government to territories where it has not arisen naturally – and if the fundamental assumptions are right the details will, to a very large extent, come out right as well. An example of the wrong sort of assumption is provided in the following item from *The Guardian*.

'VOMIT DRUG' PLAN FOR THUGS

A doctor of philosophy has evolved a new plan for dealing with violent criminals. It involves the use by the Courts of 'aversion therapy', one method of which would be repeatedly to give an offender a drug causing violent nausea while showing him things connected with his offence.

The drug is the 'potent and very unpleasant' apomorphine, based on opium, which has been used in the treatment of sexual perverts and alcoholics.

The man who thinks Courts should have the power to order its use is Dr J. Kay, who expresses his views in an article in *Justice of the Peace and Local Government Review*. He states: Upon finding the accused guilty of the crime of violence, whatever its legal classification, the remand would be ordered with the view of determining by psychological investigations, the extent and the depth of the problem and the proposed intensity of required treatment.' Dr Kay goes on: 'Should this idea raise some moral doubts, let us state here that in the struggle of society against its violent enemies, the guilty offenders are expendable, society is not.'[10]

This is the sort of thinking that is dangerous, for a society in which anybody at all is 'expendable' is a society that is not worth defending. Dr Kay is a victim of the myth that there is something called 'society' which is more important than the people in it. This kind of thinking can, however, be found as much within the bounds of retributive penal theory as within the bounds of the 'treatment' theory.

The second safeguard for the offender is that the best ways of helping people generally depend on having their co-operation – such as various forms of analysis and group therapy – and also that it will probably be cheaper to treat most offenders on an outpatient basis rather than to shut them up in institutions. For many first offenders, as we have already noted, the shock of proceedings being taken, together with a fine, seems to be sufficient 'treatment'.

Thirdly, there would, of course, have still to be some access to the Courts by way of appeal against whatever treatment might be decided upon; and the Courts will still need to establish the facts of the case in the first instance. What precisely would be the best form of consultation between the Courts and the various specialists about the treatment would have to be worked out by trial and error. Some people prefer the idea of a separate sentencing panel to decide upon the treatment required, others prefer that the specialists should merely advise the judge. Either way there should probably still be a right of final appeal through the Courts, for there is good precedent for supposing that it is the Courts that are the best defenders of civil liberty. The building up and testing of new institutions for penal treatment will not be a quick or easy job, but it is one that we ought to begin, and perhaps are beginning.

The Trouble with John Doe

Anyone who sets out to consider the needs of the criminal offender is liable to be accused of having more sympathy with the criminal than with his victims. The short answer is that we have to have sympathy with both – but that the victim is not helped by more violence being done in his name. The offender in fact claims more of our attention because he is the one who is in greater need of help

[10] *The Guardian*, 30 December, 1963.

(by and large), and because he is the one whose rights are more in danger of being overlooked.

The outstanding feature of anti-social behaviour is not its moral wickedness but the extent to which it is a product of the way a person has been treated by others; and when all has been said and done there remains the fundamental question of how far the goals of our society themselves contribute to crime. It is certain that the present patterns of crime have something to do with our living in a changing society and it is not impossible that our present level of crime is also the price we pay for living in a competitive society. A society which values very highly the qualities of thrustingness, acquisitiveness and competitiveness is not providing a very good model of human behaviour. The trouble with John Doe is not only in himself but also in the fact that he was born into, and brought up in, this particular society, and to that extent it is not John Doe, but we ourselves, that should be weighed in the balance.

Moral responsibility in this context is a matter of attempting to counter the adverse influences which exist in society by a concern for other people which is active, informed, realistic and generous. We are being 'responsible' when we care deeply about John Doe and what happens to him. So long as we live together in society we cannot get away from interfering in other people's lives, but we can do much more than we are yet doing to ensure that the interference is effected in the way which does the most real good and the least real harm. To give the last word to the New Testament: 'See to it that no one pays back wrong for wrong, but always aim at doing the best you can for each other and for all men' (I Thess. 5.15).

5

THE RIGHT TO LIFE

It is absurd but true to say that we do not know exactly what we mean by the words 'human' and 'life'. So far as 'life' is concerned, there is no gap between living matter and non-living molecules: living matter is simply matter organized in a particular way (*see* A. R. Peacocke, 'The Molecular Organisation of Life' in *Biology and Personality* edited by Ian T. Ramsey, Oxford: Blackwell, 1965). Equally, there is no single, unambiguous point at which we can say that a person is 'dead'. So far as 'human' is concerned, no clear gap has been established between man and other animals (for the different positions *see Biology and Personality*, especially the papers by Dr David Lack, 'Natural Selection and Human Nature', Professor Maynard Smith, 'An Agnostic View of Evolution', and Sir Alister Hardy, 'Another View of Evolution'), there is no single, unambiguous point in the processes of conception, pregnancy and birth at which we can say that we are dealing with 'a human being' rather than 'a foetus' and there is no simple definition by which we can say that the entity which is born, if it should happen to be deformed, is 'a human being' or 'a monster'. These difficulties of definition lie behind the moral problems of abortion and euthanasia and they raise in an acute form the fundamental question of all moral discussion: what is the value of a human being?

The Quality of Human Life

The humanist view is that the value of human life depends on its quality and in humanist discussions of abortion and euthanasia there appears from time to time the phrase 'quality of life' with a suggestion, made very guardedly, that some kinds of human life are worth preserving and some are not. In *The Sanctity of Life and the Criminal Law* Dr Glanville Williams writes:

It is good that men should feel a horror of taking human life, but in a rational judgement the quality of the life must be considered. The absolute interdiction of suicide and euthanasia involves the impossible assertion that every life, no matter what its quality or circumstances, is worth living and obligatory to be lived. This assertion of the value of mere existence, in the absence of all the activities that give meaning to life, and in the face of the disintegration of personality that so often follows from prolonged agony, will not stand scrutiny. On any rationally acceptable philosophy there is no ethical value in living any sort of life: the only life that is worth living is the good life.[1]

The things which make the 'good life' are presumably the physical enjoyments of hearing, seeing, tasting, smelling, touching and moving, the social pleasures, from conversation to marriage and parenthood, the intellectual pleasures of the use of reason, and the moral pleasures of the acquisition and the exercise of virtue. No one human being enjoys every one of these to the full, and such complete exercise is not necessary in order to have a life which is worth living. Humanists are not very precise about the point at which impairment of the faculties renders a person ineligible for the good life but they believe that such a point exists. Somewhere we must draw the line and say, 'Below this life is not worth living and ought to be brought to an end – or not allowed to begin'.

If God exists, this list of the elements of the 'good life' omits the most important of all, and the only one which is essential, which is the knowledge of God and of this world as his world. This is the difference between Christians and humanists that no amount of argument or reasoning can remove. To the Christian what matters is not the degree of physical or mental activity that is possible, but the quality of personality that is present and the chance of making a response to God. Even when we cannot communicate with a person we are not entitled to assume that a personality does not exist; we do not know what inner activities are taking place, but we do not thereby establish that there are no activities, or that the person would be better off if the activities were brought to an end. The fact is that physical and mental disabilities have very little to do with character or with happiness: there are people in possession of all their faculties who seem to be very unhappy indeed and people in possession of very few faculties who give an impression of considerable happiness and are very much loved by those around them.

---

[1] Glanville Williams, *The Sanctity of Life and the Criminal Law* (London: Faber & Faber, 1958), pp. 281–2.

The Christian argument, like the humanist argument, stands or falls by the facts, and one event in particular in recent years – the international medical tragedy of the use of the drug thalidomide – has focused our attention on the facts of deformity and the 'quality of life'.

The Thalidomide Babies

In 1961 the drug thalidomide, first synthesized in 1956 and widely used as a tranquillizer for pregnant women, was found to be the cause of a sudden increase in the number of babies born with deformities. West Germany was the first country to use the drug and the first to withdraw it (in November, 1961), and the nature and scale of the problem that had arisen there may be estimated from the following statement reported in *The Guardian*:

Among affected cases the commonest defect is phocomelia, a term used to describe short hands and feet near the shoulders and hip joints, which resemble the flippers of a seal. At Dr Hepp's hospital alone 515 cases of this kind have already been encountered, and many more continue to present themselves there and elsewhere in Western Germany for treatment.[2]

The Ministry of Health estimated that in England and Wales in 1964 there were about 250–300 children alive with thalidomide induced malformations.[3]

The public response to this event may be illustrated by quotations from two letters carried by *The Guardian*. The first reads:

Sir, – I am shocked by your comment and by the weight of public unfeeling which is crushing Lady Summerskill's brave attempt to stop the limbless babies being condemned to life. Of all the pious crimes committed during the course of history in the name of religion this refusal to grant the mercy of oblivion must be the most horrible and unnatural. . . . What a strange topsyturvy society it is where the young and healthy are discouraged from having children and the diseased and unfit are forced to bring cripples and monsters into the world.[4]

The opposite point of view was put in the other letter printed immediately below:

. . . I am teaching at a school where several children are without legs, arms,

---

[2] *The Guardian*, 28 July, 1962.
[3] Ministry of Health, *Deformities Caused by Thalidomide* (London: H.M.S.O., 1965), p. 49.
[4] *The Guardian*, 26 July, 1962.

or are otherwise incapable of making full use of their limbs. All these children are capable of getting a great deal from life and many people are prepared to devote their lives to making this possible.

No man can make the decision that this child shall live and this child shall die. It would be grossly wrong to expect any doctor to make such a decision. Maybe if some of those who consider it right to throw away these children, as if they were pieces of chipped pottery, were to visit the places where such children are trained to live a full and useful life, they might think again.

This second letter points to one of the key facts in the argument, that ideas about 'the mercy of oblivion' are not shared by those who actually deal with deformed children. The article in *The Guardian* by the medical correspondent Dr Alfred Byrne, from which we have already quoted, also says:

West German doctors are meeting with striking success in their efforts to make life practicable for the first babies born with faulty or missing limbs after the mothers had taken thalidomide during early pregnancy.

Their achievements can be judged from the case-history of a Heidelberg doctor's daughter born without arms but with one little finger sprouting from her right shoulder: she is now playing the dulcimer at the age of two years.

Specialists at Heidelberg University orthopaedic clinic trained her first to develop her sense of touch, her muscle power and dexterity until she learned how to hold small articles such as a lead pencil between the finger tip and armpit. Shortly afterwards they fitted her with two plastic shells and a shoulder harness until she became used to wearing them. Then they added artificial, 'pneumatic' arms which are made to move by the action of compressed carbon dioxide gas.

By using only her finger to release valves that produce turntable movements above the elbows, the girl now holds the hammer for her instrument in both mittens in order to tinkle out a tune. In playing she uses her equipment without conscious effort, ignoring the mittens to concentrate on the keyboard. Similarly, when throwing the hospital's 'medicine ball' she uses the artificial hands as though they were part of herself.

At a recent study course held by the British Council for Rehabilitation of the Disabled, Professor Oskar Hepp said that 'this charming child learned to handle her prostheses in an amazingly short time'. Her aptitude is shared by most of the infants surviving in this group. According to the speaker, they are above normal intelligence, with eyes that are bright and observant even when shining from disfigured faces. 'One cannot doubt the quality of their personalities', said Dr Hepp, who is the director of the University of Munster orthopaedic clinic.[5]

[5] *The Guardian*, 28 July, 1962.

Similarly, the Ministry of Health report, after noting some of the difficulties that have to be overcome, and special provisions that have to be made, concludes: 'Nevertheless, there is good reason to anticipate that the majority of these children will be able to enjoy a happy and stimulating childhood, to undertake a full course of education and training and later to obtain suitable employment.'[6]

The facts of disablement provide no grounds for saying that there is any level at which life is not worth living. Those who believe that some human beings can be written off, and that they are in a position to judge who they should be, are treading a dangerous road, at the end of which we can all be devalued. There are arguments to be put forward in favour of both abortion and euthanasia, but they cannot be made to depend on the question of 'the quality of life' alone.

Abortion

Abortion is like contraception in that it is essentially a matter of preventing the birth of a complete, independent human being; but it differs from contraception in that the foetus is a life which already exists, however incomplete and dependent it may be, and therefore has rights which demand some recognition. But it seems reasonable to suggest that the question of abortion does not concern a 'child' or a 'person': can there be any point short of the actual live birth at which we can confidently say that the child is a separate person? Certainly the latest stage at which an abortion can safely be performed is well short of the earliest stage at which a child can be delivered and live. What the 'rights' of a foetus may be is problematical.

Medical evidence about the operation shows that on the one hand there are some circumstances under which it is generally recognized in the medical profession that a pregnancy should be terminated: where there is a serious threat to the mother's life, or to her physical or mental health, or when a pregnancy may result after a child has been criminally assaulted. On the other hand, the evidence is not unanimous about the physical and psychological risks involved in the operation; the Royal College of Obstetricians and Gynaecologists has recorded the opinion that the risks, even for a relatively healthy woman, are considerable (British Medical Journal, 1 April, 1966). When the pregnancy creates a serious threat to the life or well-being

[6] Ministry of Health, *Deformities . . .*, p. 10.

of the mother, the moral argument is simple: the mother is a person who already has a substantial existence in the world, and she has a husband and perhaps other children to look after. Her death or mental or physical deterioration would have more serious effects on others (including the child about to be born), than would the aborting of the foetus. If the choice has to be made, whatever claims the foetus may have cannot outweigh those of the mother and the rest of the family.

The morally difficult question arises when an abortion is suggested either because the child may be deformed, or because the family may be in some way inadequate to support it, or because the mother simply does not want the child. Here there are two major principles to consider.

The first is that there is a general presumption that a pregnancy, once begun, should go to full term. The rights of the foetus may be only incipient or potential, but at the very least the existence of the foetus creates a demand on us that this life should be allowed to continue. This is true even if there is a strong expectation that the child may be deformed, because, as we have seen, the fact of deformity in itself does not give us much information about the 'quality of life' that the person is likely to enjoy. This principle is strongly reinforced by the feelings of the medical profession about the operation itself, which, according to the evidence of surgeons who have performed it, is very much a matter of killing a living creature.

The second principle is that any woman seeking an abortion should be treated as a responsible human being, capable of making her own moral decisions, unless there is a definite indication to the contrary. In the report of the Church of England on abortion there is a suggestion that a permissive policy on the operation would lead to 'a widespread resort to induced abortion for no better purpose than the relief of an inconvenience'.[7] But could this be a just description of any request for an abortion? Behind any desire to terminate a pregnancy there is likely to be a whole complex of motives, psychological, social and economic. The mother herself may not know what her own motives are, or may not be able to express them, but she and no one else knows the stresses which work on her, and how far she is able to bear them. This is where the question of the capacity of the

[7] *Abortion: An Ethical Discussion*, Report of the Committee of the Church Assembly Board for Social Responsibility (London: Church Information Office, 1965), p. 20.

family to sustain another child, or to sustain a child that may be deformed, enters into the moral judgement: it is a matter primarily for the mother's decision. She and her husband are the main people concerned and it would be very difficult to say that anybody else should have the last word. Similar considerations apply to an unmarried mother. Even if we believe that abortion is wrong in itself we are not necessarily entitled to set our moral judgement against that of the mother and to prevent her from having the operation. Moral freedom includes the freedom for someone else to do what I think is wrong.

These two principles tend in opposite directions and the resolving of them in practice is extremely difficult. Perhaps it might work in this way: before an abortion is allowed the mother should be given an opportunity to explore the consequences of her decision in consultation with trained advisers and she should be assured of any practical help that she would need if she should decide to continue the pregnancy; but if she still insists on an abortion, the operation should be permitted. This goes further than Lord Silkin's bill, which was first presented to Parliament in 1965, and a good deal further than the recommendations of the report *Abortion*.[8]

It may be noted that even so permissive a policy as this would be unlikely to eliminate illegal, 'back-street' abortions, since some woman might be reluctant to face the 'trained advisers', and might prefer the speed and secrecy of the illegal operation: the experience of, among others, Sweden and Hungary tends to support this view.[9]

There are, however, two objections to the implementation of such a policy. The first is that many, and perhaps most, members of the medical profession have deep objections, medical and moral, to a wholly permissive policy on the operation, and the moral right of a doctor not to be involved in performing an abortion has to be weighed against the moral right of a woman not to carry the child she has conceived. The second is that evidence from abroad suggests that a permissive policy on abortion might lead to a very steep rise in the demand for the operation[10] and that the National Health Service might be unable to cope with this demand – or be able to cope with it only at the expense of other parts of the service.

These doubts, together with those already mentioned about the medical and psychological effects of the operation, tend to lead the argument back to the proposals already before Parliament, that there should be wide grounds for permitting abortion (such as those

[8] Cf. *ibid.*, pp. 61–2, 66–70.   [9] *Ibid.*, pp. 55–6.   [10] *Ibid.*, p. 52–4.

suggested on p. 73), but that it should not be provided simply on demand.

So long as we consider the subject of abortion by itself we are largely faced with a choice between two evils; the real way out of the situation in the long run is likely to be in the more effective use of contraceptive methods rather than in the strict limitation of abortions. The most hopeful possibility here might be an extension of the domiciliary service tried experimentally in Southampton and in Newcastle-upon-Tyne for those families who need contraceptive advice but are unlikely (for various reasons) to take the initiative in visiting a family planning clinic.[11] Another possibility which is relatively unexplored is that of male or female sterilization, though the latter has its own dangers: some disquiet has been expressed among social workers about the way in which mothers have been persuaded to have this operation immediately after the birth of a child, without sufficient time for consideration and consultation. In this, as in all other matters, the need to preserve individual responsibility has to be weighed against even the most pressing claims of social policy.

Euthanasia

The idea of euthanasia, of hastening the death of someone from motives of compassion, covers two main situations: (1) where someone is close to death and can be kept alive for a few more hours or days only by intensive medical care; (2) where someone may be expected to live for weeks, months, or even years, but in considerable pain or in some other circumstances such that we might say that life is not worth living for them.

The first situation is a comparatively new one, in that it is only in recent times that techniques and machines have been developed which can prolong substantially the life of a patient who is near death. The ability of modern medicine to keep people alive has gone so far that it has become necessary to set out official definitions of the state of death; the rules reported to be in use in Massachusetts General Hospital in Boston, U.S.A., are: ' . . . for "certifying brain death in association with lung and heart activity artificially sustained by mechanical aids" . . . that there has been no spontaneous breathing for at least 60 minutes; no response to any reflexes, no change in heart rate in response to

[11] Harriet Wilson, 'The Plight of the Large Family,' *New Society*, 7 April, 1966, p. 10.

certain tests; and a flat EEG (electro-encephalograph) for at least
60 minutes of continuous recording.'[12] So far as this situation is concerned, there seems to be no very obvious obligation to take extensive
steps to keep alive a person who by any common-sense standards has
reached the end of his time, and who would not live except by the
use of extensive or exceptional medical techniques (though it is not
easy to define the term 'exceptional' – *see* the report of the Church
of England: *Decisions about Life and Death*, London: Church Information Office, 1965, Appendix 4, 'Moral and Medical Distinctions
between "Ordinary" and "Extraordinary" Means', pp. 56 ff.). It
ought perhaps to be stated explicitly in the law that a doctor is not
bound in all circumstances to use all conceivable means of prolonging
a patient's life. The official reason for the use of every possible technique on patients for whom there seems, to the lay eye, to be no hope
is that we never know that there is no hope of at least a brief recovery,
but it seems reasonably certain that there are cases in which doctors
do know this, so far as anyone can be certain about anything, and in
which some doctors do withdraw, or not provide, services which
might have prolonged life a little longer, or in which they provide
drugs which relieve pain at the expense of shortening life. Some
members of the medical profession, however, would object to this
practice, or at least to the official recognition or encouragement of
it, on the ground that it would tend to impair the trust of patients in
their doctors.

The second situation, in which it is proposed to end the life of
someone who is not expected to die at once from natural causes, is
much more morally doubtful. In so far as the suggestion may be based
on the notion of the 'quality of life' experienced by the patient, we
have already considered the argument that this is an inadequate
approach to human beings, whatever their capacities. At one extreme
we may be dealing with a birth that cannot be called 'human' at all:
'On rare occasions such a monster will live. It may belong to the
fish stage of development, with vestigial gills, webbed arms and feet,
and sightless eyes.'[13]

Such a being is likely to live at most only a few hours, but many
people would feel that during this time it ought to be given ordinary
nursing care, and that such caring is not beyond the material and

[12] Abraham Marcus, 'When Is a Patient Really Dead?' *The Observer*, 15
November, 1964.
[13] Williams, *The Sanctity of Life* . . ., p. 33.

spiritual resources of our civilization, although it would be difficult to condemn anyone who took the opposite point of view in these particular circumstances. At anything less than this extreme, the bringing to an end of the life of, say, a spastic child by the deliberate refusal of the fullest medical care (for example, by not administering antibiotics during an attack of pneumonia) seems morally indefensible.

Even if the idea of bringing someone's life to an end is based on compassion for suffering, rather than on a standard for the 'quality of life', there are four objections to it. The first is that the taking of life is an act quite unlike anything else that we can do and that it requires the gravest reasons and the utmost certainty that we are in the right – and these conditions can hardly be said to hold true of the arguments in favour of euthanasia. The second is that it is by no means clear that most of those to whom this compassion is extended would welcome the suggestion of ending their lives. The third, which follows on from this, is that a general use of euthanasia would involve grave dangers of pressure by the relatives of a very sick person to assent to it; in fact the practice of euthanasia could easily cause as much distress and fear as it set out to relieve. The fourth objection is that what we call compassion can sometimes be really our own fear of the threat which the sick or disabled person presents to our own security and peace of mind, and the call he or she makes upon us which we feel unable to meet. The threat is 'This may happen to me', and the call is 'I may have to help this person, to respond to him or her in some way'. Part of the motivation behind the desire to introduce euthanasia for other people is simply lack of courage and of compassion.

The Christian refusal to accept the principle of euthanasia may seem harsh to some, but so far as the practical questions are concerned it can lay some claim to being more realistic than the opposite point of view. In a question that is surrounded by such moral doubts our respect for our fellow human beings, of every condition and capacity, is best expressed by attempting to abide by the 'natural' term of life, so far as we can see what it is: not necessarily going to the limits of medical techniques in our efforts to keep alive one who is rapidly dying; not arbitrarily withdrawing medical help from one for whom there is hope of life; and not deliberately bringing even a limited life to an end by any other means. This still leaves many difficult practical decisions to the medical profession, but it does at least maintain the fundamental principle that the right to live is the primary right of any sort of human being.

The Theology of Self-Defence

One major question about the right to life remains to be discussed: Is it permissible to kill (or to use any lesser violence) in self-defence, either as an individual, or as a nation in war? Most people would answer 'yes' to this question: if they were attacked by someone who had murderous intentions, such as an armed rebel, or an insane person, they would resist with any weapon that came to hand, and if necessary they would press their resistance to the point of killing their attacker.

There has, however, always been minority opinion, particularly among Christians, which has said that it is never right to do violence to a fellow human being, even in self-defence. At its simplest, this view is based on a direct moral perception that killing is absolutely wrong. This is something that either we see or we do not see. Most people do not see it and as we have already argued there is a need for wariness about moral absolutes.

But the refusal to take any sort of violent action against a fellow human being may be based on a different and rather stronger argument, namely, that the most effective way of dealing with the violence of other people is not to return it. The man who wants to take my life is weaker, morally, than I am, and he, of the two of us, is more in need of being looked after. If I face him with his own weapons, if I resist him by force, I am acting at his level of moral perception and not at my own: I am giving him only the same answer that he has already found for himself. If I do not resist him, then I demonstrate to him in practice that there is another way. It is, in these circumstances, the only way of showing the love of God for him which works through me and which is greater than my own self-love.

As a general argument, this is of the highest importance, both for Christian theology and for other forms of ethic, but in the specific instances of an act that the law would recognize as justifiable homicide or of national resistance to an invasion it does not quite work out. There are two difficulties that it does not meet. The first is the effect of my death on others beside myself and my attacker: to meet violence with forgiveness and courage is a good thing, but to leave a child fatherless is not a good thing. Allowing oneself to be killed is a unique

and irreversible act and would need a very large moral gain to justify
it. While it is possible that it might produce a moral gain for one's
adversary and for oneself, this is unlikely to outweigh the loss caused
to a wife and children, or to the community at large. This is also the
difficulty for pacifism at a national level: non-resistance is not effective
unless it is voluntary, and while an entirely pacifist nation is conceivable in theory, a nation cannot go pacifist by a majority vote.
The second difficulty is that the value of non-resistance probably
depends to some extent on the capacity of my opponent to perceive
the nature of my act: would I be justified in not resisting a homicidal
attacker who was insane?

The pacifist argument fails, for most of us, because it attempts to
deal with a complex moral situation by a simple moral absolute, but
it is none the less of the highest importance in that it emphasizes the
fact that all human beings, whatever they do and whatever their
moral condition, are to be treated with the same compassion and
respect that we desire for ourselves and that in treating any human
being with less respect than he can rightly claim we make ourselves
less than human. It emphasizes also the fact that the only final answer
to violence is to absorb it and not give it back, which is one of the
fundamental statements of Christianity: 'Father, forgive them; they
do not know what they are doing.' In this sense the pacifist movement
is operating from the heart of the Christian faith.[14]

The Value of Life

It is in questions of life and death that the Christian hope of eternal
life most directly translates into practical decisions which contradict
the practical decisions of those who expect nothing after death. In
many things, above all in the sense of a need for respect for man as
man, Christians and humanists are on the same side, but in the matter
of death and suffering we work from different positions to different
ends. ' . . . if Christ was not raised, then our gospel is null and void,
and so is your faith . . . But the truth is, Christ was raised to life . . .'
(I Cor. 15. 14, 20). To the Christian every event is usable and we cannot
make suffering an absolute bad because an event that poses a severe

[14] No mention has been made of capital punishment, but the views already
expressed in the chapter on 'The Criminal Law' and in this chapter would rule
out any idea of capital punishment. A detailed examination of the subject can
be found in Gerald Gardiner, *Capital Punishment as a Deterrent: and the Alternative*
(London: Gollancz, 1956).

moral demand can also call forth a great moral good. It is not necessary to be a Christian either to experience this or to see it in others. A correspondent in *The Times*, reviewing a radio programme on the effects of poliomyelitis, wrote:

> Five victims recalled how they had first succumbed to the disease, how they continued living, or partly living, and how, to their capacity, they had returned to the everyday world, or adjusted themselves to a hospital future. What struck one most was their lack of self-pity, their indomitable humour, and what can only be called their transcendant humanity. Illness of this magnitude either makes or destroys; and here, one felt, the trivial had not only been cast off, it had been replaced by real philosophy.[15]

Equally, no Christian would claim that all suffering is beneficial, or that we ought to do anything less than our utmost to prevent or to relieve it; but what we do say is that the absence of suffering is not the measure by which human life is to be judged.

The value of life depends not on what happens to us, but on what we make of it, or rather on what we allow God to lead us to make of it. Life is coming to know God in himself and in others, and letting his love for us and for others work through in our lives. It is by this and by nothing else that we can measure either 'value' or 'happiness' in human beings. This growth in holiness, in love for God and for his world, has nothing to do with our physical or mental capacities: the quality of our life depends upon our moral nature.

[15] 'Notes on Broadcasting', *The Times*, 28 July, 1962.

6

MEN, WOMEN AND CHILDREN

THERE are few areas of moral theology that rouse as much emotion as that which deals with sexual relationships: marriage, the family, divorce, illegitimacy and homosexuality. There can also be few areas of moral theology – or indeed of any study – in which so many general statements are made with so little attention to the evidence. 'Cry Havoc' seems to be the common attitude. But what evidence there is about current sexual behaviour does not support a cry of havoc. What moralists ought rather to be concerned about is the relationship between our present social institutions and the real moral, emotional and physical well-being of men, women and children – the way in which social institutions and moral conventions help or hinder the development and continuance of good personal relationships. Here we might at times rightly cry havoc.

The Family

Let us begin with a story which speaks for itself. On 3 February, 1965, *The Times* carried the following report:

FEW COMFORTS IN HOME FOR HOMELESS
West Malling, Kent, Feb. 2

A mile or so up the road from this attractive village in a hostel – a former R.A.F. camp – live 28 homeless families. Even in the unaccustomed February sunshine it is not an attractive place, yet to compare it to a concentration camp, as Mr Lubbock, M.P. for Orpington, did recently, is going a bit too far.

Angered by Mr Lubbock's accusations and basking in the warm glow of the Minister of Health's approval of the hostel, Kent County Council today invited journalists to have a look for themselves. They took the precaution of warning them that they deliberately avoided making the place too attractive 'otherwise people would be tempted to stay'.

They have succeeded fairly well. Mrs Latz, for instance, has to find room for herself and nine children in two bedrooms. The beds are jammed next to one another without a space between. Mrs Bush, however, has three bedrooms for herself and one boy, aged 12.

ONE QUARTER

The official explanation is that Mrs Latz's 'quarter' is the only one with large enough bedrooms. Although the hostel is less than half full, it would not do apparently to give the large families more than one 'quarter', as the children would not like to be separated from their mother at night.

On the whole the place is clean enough. Several of the residents this morning were hard at work with mops and pails. This, we were assured, was not a 'bull' session but everyday routine. The bathrooms and lavatories were well looked after and there was nothing to support Mr Lubbock's allegation that children paddled through open sewers.

The chief complaint was that a family are allowed to stay for only three months at a time. If they have not found a house by then the children are separated from their parents and put into a home. For Mrs Latz, whose husband has not been able to work for the past 10 years because of ill-health, there is little hope of finding anything.

HUSBANDS BARRED

Most women resent being separated from their husbands, who are not allowed to live on the premises, can visit their families only at week-ends, and must leave by 8 p.m. For the younger wives, such as the attractive blonde girl living with two small children in a grubby room pathetically decorated with cut-out pictures of the Beatles and the Rolling Stones, this seems an unnecessary hardship.

But, council officials say, the husband must continue to live in the district in order to keep his name on the housing list. And, they add, some of the 'husbands' are not really husbands at all. Life is not much fun if you are without a home.

On 20 November, 1965, *The Guardian* reported: 'Two husbands who defied a High Court order by sleeping at the Kent County Council hostel for homeless families at West Malling last week-end were sent to prison yesterday for contempt of court. No period of sentence named, subject to five judges' discretions.'

By Christmas 1965 the matter had attracted national attention, and there was a protest march on Westminster and an appeal for funds by a newly-formed Association of Friends of the Homeless Families.

On 7 April 1966, after the general election, *The Guardian* reported that the residents' committee had written to the Prime Minister and received a friendly reply: 'It is indeed the individual, and particularly the family, that the social services should seek to help.'

On 3 May, 1966, Kent County Council secured a possession order in the High Court against one of the families, on the grounds that they had ignored the County Council's rule that families must normally leave after three months.[1]

Families may find themselves homeless through no fault of their own. In a background article on the problem, *The Guardian* quoted the case of one of the families at the West Malling hostel:

The father, Joe, is 32, the mother, Joan, 29, with three boys aged 6 years, 5 years, and 6 months, and three girls aged 8, 4, and 2 years.

At Sheerness, Mr Gibbons worked as a labourer at the paper mills for a few years, earning about £9 a week. They rented a "two-down, two-up" terrace house in Sheerness, which being in a poor state of repair and over-crowded was never in show-house condition. Somehow they managed for five years without getting into debt. People who met them in those days said the children seemed to love their parents and they in turn thought the world of the children.

Then the owner of the house died and the executors decided to sell it with vacant possession. The Gibbonses were told to get out. They applied to Sheerness Urban District Council for housing, but were told that none was available. (Mrs Gibbons is a local girl who, as Sheppey people say, had 'never been off the island'.) They could find no rented accommodation at anything near the price they could afford, and so they were evicted and arrived at King Hill.[2]

When a family is evicted from the hostel, as *The Times* noted in the report quoted above, the children are split from the parents – in 1964, thirty families, involving about 100 children, passing through the hostel were thus split at the end of their three months stay. The 1966 report of the Children's Department of the Home Office shows 1,727 children taken into care between 31 March, 1964, and 31 March, 1965, through homelessness following eviction, and 1,323 children who came into care in the same period because the family was home-less for other reasons (the total number of children in care for all reasons in England and Wales in 1965 was 67,099). This is, of course, apart from any moral considerations, bad economics. At the time of writing Berkshire County Council, having evicted a family with

[1] *The Guardian*, 4 May, 1966.
[2] 'Test Case Ruling May Split Family,' *The Guardian*, 5 January, 1966.

eight children for being in arrears with the rent, are paying over £30 a week to place the children with foster parents – a sum considerably larger than would be needed to buy a house for the family and present it to them free of charge.

Morally the present procedure is indefensible. In a land in which respect for the family has for centuries been considered both a Christian and a civic virtue we might expect more than a passing sense of astonishment that public bodies, in dealing with families that are homeless because of the scarcity of housing, or because of a failure to budget properly – and with six children, on the wage of an un-skilled man, it requires a miracle to budget properly – should see fit at the very outset to separate a father from his children and from his wife and at the end of a further three months should encourage the homeless by separating the children from their mother. If this were a punishment imposed on the family for some misdeed, it would be considered savage and excessive, but since it is the result of administra-tive action it seems to be all right. Our respect for the family disappears remarkably easily before our desire for administrative convenience, or our reluctance to raise the rates, or the fact that the family appears to be 'feckless' (we do not, of course, inquire very deeply into the con-ditions underlying fecklessness), or the possibility that the fathers and mothers of children may not be legally married. One might be tempted to suppose that the real crime of these people is the gravest of all in our society: *they have failed to acquire property*.

This particular scandal has begun to receive so much attention that we may hope that it may soon be set right and that the organs of society will realize that their first duty is to house a family together – even a family that cannot pay the rent – but, the moral insensitiveness that lies behind the King Hill hostel story and the similar actions of housing authorities and welfare authorities throughout the country will not disappear. It is not so long ago that officials of a Children's Department literally kidnapped two children while their mother was out of the house and held them prisoner in a children's home. The *casus belli* was the fact that the mother was refusing to send the children to school, claiming that she was competent to educate them herself at home. The officials were acting under a court order, and the mother eventually lost her case – but what sort of a concept of welfare was expressed by kidnapping? In another case early in 1966 only a national newspaper campaign, the personal intervention of the Home Secretary and the uncommon good sense and willingness to break the rules of the local Children's Committee and Department rescued a little girl from a home to which she had been committed in furtherance of a dispute between her mother and her headmaster.

Such solutions to administrative problems will go on, because of two reactions which are deeply engrained in all of us. The first is punitive: 'This person is being difficult. He/she must be taught a lesson'. The second is defensive: 'This is what the book says', 'It is the policy of the Department', 'I am here to administer the law'. What we constantly need are people who are prepared to defy the book, the policy, and if necessary the law, in order to serve the real needs of human beings; and people who are sufficiently free in themselves to have no need to punish others. In short, people who are prepared to stand up for the love of God. The bond between father and mother and child, in particular, still needs a lot of defending.

Marriage

What value are we to assign to the relationship between a man and a woman? The Old Testament contains one of the finest love songs in any literature – the Song of Songs:

> As a lily among thorns,
> So is my love among the daughters.
> As the apple tree among the trees of the wood,
> So is my beloved among the sons.
> I sat down under his shadow with great delight,
> And his fruit was sweet to my taste.
> He brought me to the banqueting house,
> And his banner over me was love (2.2–4).

The Old Testament view of marriage is one of vigorous and unashamed enjoyment as is evidenced from the following quotation:

> Let thy fountain be blessed:
> And rejoice in the wife of thy youth.
> As a loving hind and a pleasant doe,
> Let her breasts satisfy thee at all times;
> And be thou ravished with her love.
> For why shouldest thou, my son, be ravished with a
>   strange woman,
> And embrace the bosom of a stranger?
> For the ways of man are before the eyes of the Lord,
> And he weigheth carefully all his paths (Prov. 5.18–21).

The oldest stratum of Genesis contains a hint of the nature of the union between man and woman – 'Therefore shall a man leave his father and his mother, and shall cleave unto his wife: and they shall be one flesh' (2.24) – but in practice the people of the Old Testament were not strictly monogamous.

The New Testament opts firmly for one particular view of marriage: that essentially it is a matter of one man and one woman being joined together for life. The choice is based on the belief that only this union can offer the full development of the affection, understanding and security between these two human beings. It is not that God has promulgated a law saying that marriage shall be like this, but rather that we find the nature of human beings to be such that this is the way to happiness. As a point of observation this may be incorrect, but as a view of marriage it is widely held, not only by Christians but also by others – at least some sociologists would agree with it. In *The Family and Marriage* Ronald Fletcher writes:

Clearly there is some truth in the notion of 'falling in love' (it happens), and clearly the continuation of love in marriage is a desirable thing (it helps). But, apart from the obvious comment that marriage is for the foundation of the family, for the begetting and rearing of children, and thus entails far more than the maintenance of personal romantic feelings, all one would tentatively suggest is that perhaps love also has other qualities; that it is perhaps something which can grow and become more profound and satisfying as ordinary problems, difficulties, duties are shared, as mutual concern for children is experienced, as qualities of character come to be more deeply appreciated.[3]

But the New Testament also regards marriage as a life-long union because it sees marriage in the context of God's love for the human race. The New Testament holds that the love which a man and a woman have for each other is a part of the love that God has for each of them and their love is a mark of God's love in them. Every human act of love is a movement towards knowing God, and the union of a man and a woman is the image of the union between Christ and his Church.

This is not a high ideal but the normal attainment of ordinary men and women who enter into marriage. If Christian marriage were a 'high ideal' it would not be worth talking about. The defensive barriers which we erect around marriage by our attitude to divorce, illegitimacy and pre-marital intercourse are not really necessary

[3] Ronald Fletcher, *The Family and Marriage* (London: Penguin Books, 1962), p. 133.

because marriage does not need this kind of defence: it is too strong
and attractive and deep an experience to need our worrying over it.

Pre-marital Sexual Intercourse and Illegitimacy

One out of every 16 children born now in England and Wales is illegitimate.
For the children of mothers under 20 the number is one out of every four.

Unmarried mothers are giving birth to a vast new population of 55,000
babies a year in Britain.

Unmarried mothers begin at 13, give birth to their maximum number of
babies at the age of 23 (more than five a day), subside slowly through the
thirties and forties till there are about eight illegitimate children a year born
to women over 50.

Unmarried mothers come from every class and background. One third
of all our babies are now *conceived* out of wedlock.[4]

The figures in this quotation are those for 1961; by 1964, the latest
year for which figures were available at the time of writing, the
number of illegitimate live births had risen to 63,340 out of a total
of 875,972 live births.[5] The effect of statistics of course varies according
to the way in which they are presented, and if we express the same
facts by saying that in 1964 over 92% of babies were born in wedlock,
it becomes clear that this is not exactly a problem that threatens the
foundations of married life. Again, the 1964 figure represents 1.3 illegitimate live births per 1,000 of the total population of England and
Wales, but in the decade 1851–60, the first period for which figures
are available, the rate was 2.2 per 1,000. It is also clear that this problem
is not primarily a matter of the behaviour of teenagers: the peak age
in 1961 was 23, and nearly a quarter of the illegitimate births were to
women between the ages of 30 and 50.

The immediate practical problem which is posed by the 63,340
illegitimate babies born in 1963 and their successors in subsequent
years is that of finding ways of making life tolerable for those mothers
and their babies who are not supported by their own families. In a
second article on the subject, Jeremy Sandford wrote:

No girl is the same after having a baby. Whatever their attitudes before
they have had them, these one-out-of-16 mothers are almost always com-

[4] Jeremy Sandford, 'Who Are the Unmarried Mothers and Fathers?' *The
Observer*, 5 May, 1963.
[5] *The Statistical Review for England and Wales, 1964*, Part II, *Population* (London:
H.M.S.O., 1966).

mitted to their babies from the moment that they actually hold them in their arms. Yet, for those who want to keep their babies, life in Britain is weighted against them.

In Denmark, 93 per cent of all unmarried mothers keep their babies. In Britain only a few more than half are able to do so. About 20,000 give their babies away.[6]

The practical steps which he suggested are:

... hostels to live in with their babies (the L.C.C. has two); flatlets or bedsits grouped together so that they can help one another; training courses, like those available to all unmarried mothers in Denmark; an employment agency to find them jobs; foster-parents who will volunteer to look after a girl till she's on her feet; a more efficient method of getting maintenance from the fathers.[7]

Until we make it possible for every mother of an illegitimate child to go through her confinement in comfort and in an atmosphere of friendliness, and provide her with a place to live and means of support after the birth of her child for as long as she needs them, we shall not be in any position to generalize about what the mothers themselves think about the choice between keeping the child or having it adopted; the fact that at present economic and social pressures leave so many mothers no choice in the matter is a much more serious moral weakness in our society than the size of the illegitimate birth rate.

The most practical step of all, of course, would be the prevention of illegitimate births and half a step towards this would be to provide contraceptive advice for unmarried people. This raises the spectre of 'encouraging promiscuity', but the plain fact is that the alternatives are not contraceptive advice or chastity, but contraceptive advice or intercourse without the benefits of contraception. Those who take what they consider to be a moral stand against giving contraceptive advice to the unmarried are really increasing the number of abortions and illegitimate births – which is neither practical nor moral. But even freely-available contraceptive advice would not solve the problem, because precautions are not always what people want to take, either because they do not like contraceptives, or because taking the risk of conceiving a child is an act of defiance, or because the intercourse is unpremeditated: ignorance about birth or birth control probably accounts for only a small proportion of illegitimate pregnancies.

The moral problem posed by the figures for conceptions outside

[6] Sandford, *The Observer*, 12 May, 1963.   [7] *Ibid.*

marriage is much more one of pre-marital sexual intercourse than of
sexual promiscuity. While one birth in sixteen is illegitimate, one in
three begins outside marriage. In a study of 1,873 boys and girls
between the ages of fifteen and nineteen published in 1965, it was
found that only 12% of the girls in the whole sample had experienced
the full act of sexual intercourse, but that 'among the girls who were
engaged, 37 per cent were having sexual intercourse with their
fiancés'.[8] The author comments:

> In addition to the engaged couples who decide to have sexual intercourse
> before their wedding day, there are also courting couples who decide to get
> married when the girl is pregnant. This further increases the number of
> experienced teenagers who only have premarital intercourse with the person
> they will marry. It seems likely that much of the premarital sexual activities
> of teenagers is not promiscuous behaviour.[9]

There is, however, less pressure in recent years to regularize a pregnancy by marriage:

> A study of the Registrar-General's figures since 1938 on rates of illegitimacy
> and premarital conceptions taken together shows that although the illegitimacy
> rate has gone up, the percentage of teenage brides who were pregnant on their
> wedding day has gone down. Therefore the social pressures on the unmarried
> mother to marry have declined, and this decrease in the rate of premarital
> conceptions 'regularised' by marriage more than accounts for the increase in
> illegitimate births.[10]

The immediate moral question therefore is whether our objections
to sexual promiscuity (which are implied in what we have already
said about marriage) apply also to pre-marital sexual intercourse.
The morality of any sexual activity is governed by its appropriateness
to the relationship between the two people involved: the more
intimate the action, the deeper the degree of commitment and of care
for each other we should expect it to convey. The intention which the
act expresses is as important as the physical nature of the act. The moral
weakness of promiscuous sexual intercourse is that it conveys false
information: the intimacy of the act implies a depth of feeling of which
neither party, in this particular relationship, is capable. Promiscuity is
important not so much as an immoral act in itself but as a symptom
of an inability to form relationships.

[8] Michael Schofield, *The Sexual Behaviour of Young People* (London: Longmans,
Green & Co., 1965), pp. 30, 164.
[9] *Ibid.*, p. 164.   [10] *Ibid.*, p. 251.

Pre-marital sexual intercourse is different in that it can take place between two people who are deeply committed to each other and who want this commitment to last for life; the relationship of love and commitment exists before the marriage vows are exchanged and the marriage ceremony will not create it if it does not exist. But the fact remains that it is the exchange of vows that is the last and critical test of the intentions of each and that the public promise of life-long commitment is the greatest gift (in a sense) that the one can give to the other. The marriage ceremony is the step in the relationship that creates the complete intimacy which it is the function of sexual intercourse to express. Even so, the question remains one for the couple themselves to decide: this is their relationship and it is up to them to say how it should go. All that anyone else can do is to point out aspects of the relationship that they themselves may not have considered and this is a very limited function. Our fundamental moral education is conveyed by the way other people behave towards us and the results we observe of our behaviour towards them. Advice and education are not levels at which we can effectively meet the needs which are expressed by promiscuous behaviour, or influence people towards pre-marital chastity. What can influence them is our own decision to live with openness and with courage and with love, and our own respect for chastity and the marriage vow.

The Breakdown of Marriage

In 1951 the number of decrees absolute granted was 28,767; in 1960 the figure had fallen to 23,369, and in 1964 it rose again to 34,868. The reasons for the variations in the figures for divorces over the years are inevitably complex: they include changes in population structure, changes in the rate of marriage in different age-groups, and changes in legislation and the availability of legal aid. All these have to be taken into account before we can make any assumptions about changes in the social and moral climate. The rise in the figures from 1960 to 1964 may seem large, but in 1947 there were almost twice as many decrees made absolute as there were in 1964. The number of petitions filed, for divorce and for annulment, was 41,468 in 1964, against 38,382 in 1951, and the 1951 figure represented only 0.5% (5.23 per 1,000) of all married women between the ages of 20 and 49.[11] As with illegitimacy, the divorce figures involve a large number of people;

[11] *The Statistical Review* . . .; see also Fletcher, *The Family and Marriage*, pp. 136–43.

but they do not involve a very large proportion of all marriages: they certainly do not provide evidence of a decline of the family, or of a threat to the institution of marriage.

This is not to say that the present laws on divorce are ideal. Proposals for altering them raise two main points: the case for divorce by consent, and the need to protect the interests of the children in a marriage:

> If there are no children to a marriage, there seems no reason why divorce should not be by mutual consent, since no one is affected but the two partners themselves, and a mutual settlement of their affairs can be worked out. But when there are *children* to the marriage, the parents are responsible for the fulfilment of duties to their children whatever may have happened to their own personal relationship, and it is arguable that divorce here should be made very difficult indeed.[12]

The case for divorce by consent is that marriage is a contract between two persons; that as in any contract they should be free to end it when they wish; that in practice the law is already almost powerless to prevent a couple who wish to end their marriage from arranging suitable evidence of adultery; and that the moral standing of the law would be improved by the admission of divorce by consent. The moral case for divorce by consent rests on the simple basic principle of freedom of moral judgement: the more important the issue, the greater the need for freedom for the people involved in it to make their own moral decisions.

The distinction between the childless marriage and the marriage with children is important, but should not be pushed too far, because on the one hand even the childless couple need some delay to provide an opportunity for second thoughts, a chance of reconciliation, and on the other hand the children in a marriage are not really going to be helped by society forcing their parents to live together beyond the point at which they are sure they want to part. A system of divorce based on consent, but providing some delay (and some counselling) for rethinking, together with a thorough investigation of the needs of the children, would probably come closest to serving the best interests of all parties. Where one partner is unwilling to consent to a divorce the situation is more complex: the partner who wishes to continue the marriage is in the stronger moral position, but it is not clear that one partner should have the right to bind the other indefinitely; the

---

[12] Fletcher, *The Family and Marriage*, p. 135.

concept of an 'innocent' and a 'guilty' party is very dubious, both psychologically and morally – it takes two persons to make a marriage, and it takes two persons to fail to make one. The faults may appear to be all on one side, but the underlying psychological dynamics are likely to be more complex. One might, for example, ask what psychological motives impelled the 'innocent' party to make such a choice of partner in the first place?

About three-quarters of the people who have been divorced marry again. The question of divorce and remarriage is a problem for Christian theology, rather than a general social problem. The Church has always recognized that a marriage can break down, that the heart can go out of it, and it has always recognized also the possibility of a second marriage if one of the partners of a first marriage dies; but the argument against a second marriage after divorce has been that the first marriage is never completely ended, even by divorce – the parties are in a state of separation only.

As the fact that Christians are not all of one mind on this subject suggests, the interpretation of the New Testament sayings on divorce (such as Mark 10. 9, 'What God has joined together, man must not separate') is not absolutely clear, but it would be more than a little odd if these alone, out of all the moral injunctions of the Bible, were to be taken as absolute and total commandments – a method of interpretation which has not, for example, been applied to the commandment, 'Thou shalt not kill'.

The established pastoral practice of the Church of England already undermines its official views on divorce, since people who have been divorced and who have entered upon a second marriage may, under certain circumstances, be admitted to communion. It is theological double-think to say that marriage after divorce is permissible so long as it does not take place in church, or that it is not permissible, but that if it unfortunately takes place it may be forgiven. If a person does something which is wrong and is forgiven, that is the end of it until the next time he does it; but if a person is engaged in a continuous activity which is wrong, and has every intention of continuing in that activity, he is not in a fit state for forgiveness. Strong pastoral considerations have led theologians to say that people who have been divorced and married again to a different partner may, if they are suitably sorry for the way things went wrong the first time, be admitted (or readmitted) to the full life of the Christian community – but this would be quite wrong if the state of the second marriage were in itself really sinful. The only logical conclusion from the established pastoral practice of admitting people to communion who have been divorced and remarried is that remarriage after divorce is a permissible state. Faced with real pastoral needs the Church of England has recognized in practice what it is not yet ready to recognize in theory.

Homosexuality

In a heterosexual relationship the distinction between sexual acts which are valid because they convey genuine feelings and those which are not is reasonably clear and is to a large extent formalized in the social structure through the concepts of marriage and the family. In homosexual relations (of both sexes) social and moral convention forbids any sexual act – a restriction which most people of heterosexual orientation would find intolerable. In so far as a homosexual condition may be taken as a sign of emotional immaturity and an inability to form a mature heterosexual relationship this convention (though not its enforcement by law) may be justified, but it can also be argued that the pressure of social and moral convention and the threat of the law at present make it almost impossible for a homosexual relationship to develop whatever potential it may have for real commitment and depth of love. Until very recently (effectively until the publication of the Wolfenden Report in 1957) it has been difficult to discuss the subject in public in a rational way because of the strong emotions that it tends to rouse. The general sense of repugnance towards homosexual behaviour and the severity of the law on homosexual acts have made it difficult to see what the facts are. This section will largely draw on one study, *Sociological Aspects of Homosexuality*, produced by Michael Schofield in 1965. In this research Schofield compares six groups of men: fifty inmates of prisons convicted of sexual offences with boys under sixteen; fifty homosexuals who are under psychiatric treatment in a hospital or out-patient clinic and a control group of fifty non-homosexuals similarly under treatment; fifty homosexuals who have not received psychiatric treatment and who have not been convicted for homosexual offences and a control group of fifty non-homosexuals who have not received psychiatric treatment and who have not been convicted for homosexual offences. He also considers and draws together previous work done in this country and abroad.

On the hostility shown to homosexuals Schofield comments:

It is very difficult to give logical reasons for the social hostility directed towards homosexuals. The discussions in previous chapters (8, 9 and 10) have indicated that it is a mistake to assume 'rationality' when dealing with a popular prejudice like this. Attempts to change human attitudes by the presentation of facts alone are notably ineffectual. People select from the myriad of facts with which they are being constantly bombarded only those messages towards which they have an initial pre-disposition.[13]

His own study indicates that there are three different types of homosexual. The first are those who are well adjusted to their condition and do not come into contact with the law or undergo psychiatric treatment. Over a wide range of comparisons these resemble well-adjusted heterosexual men more than they resemble the other two groups of homosexuals. The second type are men who get into trouble with the law for homosexual acts with adults. These resemble men who are in prison for other offences more than they resemble the first group or the third. The third type are those who are under treatment for their sexual problems. These resemble men who are under treatment for other psychological problems (including heterosexually-oriented sexual problems) more than they resemble either the well-adjusted or the convicted homosexuals. A fourth type consists of men convicted of sexual offences against boys (and in some cases against girls as well): these differ significantly from the three previous types of homosexuals. On the basis of his own researches and the findings of other workers Schofield puts forward the following theory:

Homosexuality is a condition which in itself has only minor effects upon the development of the personality. But the attitudes, not of the homosexual, but of other people towards this condition, create a stress situation which can have a profound effect upon personality development and can lead to character deterioration of a kind which prohibits effective integration with the community.

A proportion of homosexuals are unable to withstand the pressures from outside and become social casualties. These are the homosexuals most often found in prisons and clinics. Their difficulties may take a form not directly associated with the homosexual condition, although originally caused by the social hostility shown towards homosexuality. On the other hand the homosexuals who have learnt to contend with these social pressures can become adjusted to their condition and integrated with the community. These men are hardly ever found in prisons and clinics.[14]

[13] Michael Schofield, *Sociological Aspects of Homosexuality* (London: Longmans, Green & Co., 1965), p. 205.   [14] *Ibid.*, p. 203.

Several particular points are worth noting. In the first place, homosexuality is not an illness:

> Some doctors see homosexuality as just one symptom of a neurotic condition. This study of men in the Homosexual/Patient group makes it clear that some homosexuals are neurotic and in need of psychiatric help. But this does not justify the inference that all homosexuals are sick persons and should be regarded primarily as medical problems. It is true that homosexual symptoms do occur in the course of a few recognized mental or physical illnesses, but if homosexuality itself is a pathological condition, then it must be one of the most common psychological disorders known. It would be an illness from which over a million men and probably as many women were suffering (*sc. in the U.K.*), and would constitute a far bigger health problem than cancer, heart conditions or any single disease. Lindner (1956) felt that the increasingly prevalent idea of referring to homosexuality as a sickness is part of a common approach in modern society to regard non-conformity and mental illness as synonymous.[15]

The Wolfenden Report came to the same conclusion.

Secondly, the well-adjusted homosexual (who is very much in the majority) is capable of a lasting emotional relationship with another man:

> There is no doubt that a homosexual can experience a very strong emotional attachment to another man. This intense feeling has many of the same observable features as one found in the love of a man for a woman. Many people are surprised to learn that most homosexuals seek companionship and community of interest as well as sexual satisfaction. Some homosexuals do develop relationships as loyal and as closely knit as the best kind of marriage, but they do so in the face of enormous obstacles. There are none of the factors which stabilize conventional marriage and all the social pressures tend to lead to the break-up of these friendships.[16]

Thirdly, there is no real danger of homosexual men tempting non-homosexual men into regular homosexual practices:

> The results of this research showed that the Homosexual/Other (*sc. the well-adjusted, majority group*) men were not interested in proselytism. In any case this fear that heterosexual men are always liable to succumb to homosexual temptations unless protected by the law implies that normal intercourse between man and woman is inferior in some unexplained way.[17]

Fourthly, experience before the age of seventeen provides no indication for later, adult behaviour: some men who take to homosexual

[15] *Ibid.*, p. 160.   [16] *Ibid.*, p. 112.   [17] *Ibid.*, p. 176.

behaviour in adult life do not experience it (or refuse to experience it) when young and those who do have homosexual experiences when young do not generally continue in adult life: 44% of the non-homosexual control group had at least one homosexual experience before the age of 21.[18]

Fifthly, none of the methods used to 'cure' homosexuals, from deep analysis to aversion therapy, can claim much in the way of success except with a few very carefully selected patients.[19]

At the centre of this problem is the fact that by and large the homosexual (whatever the cause of his or her condition) does not have the option of pursuing a heterosexual relationship. It cannot be said firmly and finally that in a homosexual attachment there can never be a real concern for another person, or that there can never be in such a relationship a level of commitment which might appropriately be expressed by sexual intercourse. It is difficult to see that any harm is done by such acts. Christian writers on this subject commonly refer to the power of the grace of God to help homosexuals to turn their desires into constructive asexual channels, but it is not theologically impossible to ask for the grace of God to use a homosexual relationship as a means of growing in the love of God. Perhaps the attainment of a genuinely equal and caring relationship is less likely for a homosexual than for a heterosexual person and there may be biological as well as moral reasons for thinking that a homosexual relationship is unlikely to equal in full the love and security of marriage, but this is not to say that the relationship itself cannot be good. In any case we cannot accurately make this sort of inter-personal comparison. Public opinion is beginning to change on the subject of homosexuality, as current efforts to change the law show, and it is perhaps significant of a further change that in February, 1967, the women's magazine *Nova* carried an article on the situation in Holland (where adult homosexual relationships are legal and to some extent tolerated) which ended with the words: 'Giving the homosexual more freedom will mean the beginning of our own freedom to understand him and ourselves; it will help to create the only climate in which we should want to live: a climate in which we can learn.'[20] This is not the sole definition of a healthy society, but it is an important element in it.

[18] *Ibid.*, p. 135.   [19] *Ibid.*, pp. 162–72.
[20] Irma Kurz, 'Homosexuality – the Unlocking of a Law', *Nova*, February, 1967, p. 25.

D

As we have already noted, Schofield found that the group of men who were convicted of sexual offences with boys under sixteen differed markedly from the three homosexual groups (though he suggests that the replies from this group are probably less reliable than those from the other groups because of the nature of the offence – which rouses great hostility among other prisoners – and because of a sense of shame about their actions). The men in the paedophiliac group were more likely to feel guilty about their activities and to desire treatment and they more often went out of their way to avoid temptation. They tended to be older, more of them were married and more of them claimed to prefer heterosexual activities than in the homosexual groups. Fourteen out of the fifty admitted to the researcher that they had also committed offences against girls under sixteen. Over half the paedophiliac group had not had homosexual experiences themselves before the age of sixteen and they tended to have their first homosexual experiences later in life than the other groups. Schofield suggests that 'some men develop a sexual interest in boys when they are no longer obtaining heterosexual experiences'.[21]

Two points can be made in defence of the paedophiliac. The first is that assaults on children are generally at the level of sexuality appropriate to the child rather than that appropriate to the adult (that is to say, they tend to be the sort of actions which the child might easily have performed with another of the same age). The second is that the actions often take place with the co-operation of, and sometimes even at the invitation of, the child.[22] Schofield comments: 'In the paedophiliac situation it is usually assumed that the boy is the less experienced partner, but this may not always be the case. Bender and Blau (1937) state that the boy is often the initiator, and many of the Paedophiliac/Convicted men were relatively inexperienced.'[23] Assaults on children tend to involve not only an emotionally deprived adult but also an emotionally deprived child. Indeed, they may involve an innocent adult and a difficult child:

There are signs that occasionally the innocent may be convicted. It is known that some boys actively seek older men. Revitch and Weiss (1962) report

[21] Schofield, *Sociological Aspects* . . ., p. 58.
[22] Lindy Burton, 'The Assaulted Child,' *New Society*, 20 May, 1965. A previous article by the same author, 'The Child in a Road Accident,' 6 May, 1965, shows how emotional relationships may predispose a child to involvement in accidents – an idea that may seem at first sight even more far-fetched than a child's predisposition to be the victim of a sexual assault.
[23] Schofield, *Sociological Aspects* . . ., p. 60.

that the paedophiliacs' victims are usually known to be aggressive and seductive children. An American professor of law (Ploscowe, 1960) writes: 'Complaints of sex offences are easily made. They spring from a variety of motives and reasons. The psychiatrist and the psychoanalyst would have a field day were he to examine all the complaints of rape, sexual tampering with children, incest, homosexual behaviour with young boys, deviant sex behaviour, etc., in any given community. He would find that complaints are too often made of sexual misbehaviour that has occurred only in the overripe fantasies of the so-called victims. Frequently, the more or less unconscious wish for the sexual experience is converted into the experience itself. Sometimes, too, the so-called victim will charge not the one with whom he or she has had sexual experience, but someone else who is entirely innocent.'[24]

Clearly a sexual assault on a child is wrong and paedophiliacs have to be restrained. But we need to keep a sense of proportion about this offence. The technical definition of an assault is very wide:

An indecent assault in law can be committed without violence or physical harm being done to the victim. . . . A man can be convicted of an indecent assault although his conduct does not constitute an overt homosexual act as defined in this research.

. . . .

Sometimes the action is relatively harmless and the consequences out of all proportion to the act. As Calder (1955) has shown the term 'indecent assault' can cover a wide range of behaviour. Perhaps the man only put his hand on the boy's knee, and this incident gets blown up into a much more serious sexual assault, sometimes, as is alleged, by the police putting words into the mouth of the child. Sometimes the child tells an untrue story in a fit of pique without fully realizing the consequences of what he is saying.[25]

The proof of the offence often rests on the unsupported word of a child and the sense of revulsion which this offence rouses makes it doubtful whether a man accused of the offence always gets fair treatment. The sentences imposed are often very severe in relation to what has actually been done and Schofield writes that 'the paedophiliac is punished more severely than men convicted of rape, manslaughter, first degree robbery, or assault with a deadly weapon'.[26]

Not many people would go as far as the parent quoted by J. R. Oliver in his lectures in 1932 who said that he would rather his son should have his first sexual experience with an otherwise decent schoolmaster than with a prostitute, but the point is a valid one and we perhaps ought to take this offence more calmly. Certainly we

[24] *Ibid.*, p. 153.　　[25] *Ibid.*, pp. 44–5, 153.　　[26] *Ibid.*, pp. 152–3.

should do so for the sake of the child himself: most workers are agreed that more harm can come to the child from the attitude taken by parents, teachers and other adults, and from the Court proceedings, than from the actual assault. Schofield quotes the example of Israel where the interests of the child are protected even at the risk of some guilty men being acquitted, and he concludes: 'It may be that the present legal system in this country is too concerned with settling appropriate legal retribution upon the offender and not enough concerned about the child victim.'[27]

Conclusion

The whole of Christian morality is an attempt to work out the meaning of love in action and particularly the meaning of God's love for those who are in trouble. The fundamental Christian teaching on the family is what it always is, that the holy and just and loving being of God is reflected in the life-long union between a man and a woman and in the love between them and their children. Christian marriage is the nearest that human beings can come among themselves to the love of God for man; it is the image of our relationship with Christ and indeed of the source of love itself in the divine union which we attempt to express in the idea of the holy Trinity. But the quality of this relationship of marriage (and of all human relationships) is as important as its outward form: which is to say that we ought to be more shocked by an act that breaks up a family than by the fact that a father and mother are not legally married; that we ought to be more grieved by the lack of love for one another of a married couple than by an engaged couple developing their love in sexual intercourse; and that we ought to be more grieved for someone who does not love at all than for two persons of the same sex who are in love.

The fact that it is love that drives us on means that the quality of our response to any human condition matters as much as the condition to which we are responding; the value of our own morality stands or falls by the extent to which it enables us to answer to human weakness with compassion. Love also requires a free response from the other – we cannot force others to love – and it requires that we allow other people the responsibility of deciding their own actions, even when this leads to decisions of which we disapprove.

Many people fear that 'moral freedom' may mean 'moral licence',

[27] *Ibid.*, p. 152.

but such a fear suggests rather little trust in the power of the love of God and a curiously faint-hearted estimate of the attractiveness of what is good. It suggests also a failure to understand that when people act in an immoral way – provided that it really is immoral when measured against the being of God, and not just by our standards – they do so, on the whole, because they are lost, troubled and lonely and not because they find immorality more attractive. There is, in any case, no evidence of a moral decline at the present time. Many people have their own impressions about the moral state of our society, but impressions are not evidence. In his foreword to Michael Schofield's book, *The Sexual Behaviour of Young People*, Sir Herbert Broadley says: 'It is impossible to say how the behaviour of today's younger generation compares with that of the past. Unfortunately, no survey comparable with the present one has ever been undertaken before.'[28] So far as the family itself is concerned, Ronald Fletcher concludes his survey with the words:

All in all, however, I would like to end this book by reiterating my conclusion that our analysis does clearly point out that the family in contemporary Britain has not declined in nature or importance as a social institution; that its characteristics do not warrant at all the charge of 'moral decline'; and that no good end will be served by any falsely conceived and backward-looking judgements and policies.[29]

Certainly there have been some moral changes: we have more freedom now to talk about sexual matters (which is an advance rather than a decline) and possibly there is less chastity about (though this is not certain), but the major moral change of modern times is the increase in concern for the poor and the weak and the emphasis on the value of the life of every family, which is implicit in the whole concept of the welfare state and which is a gain so immense that on its own it entitles us to say that we live in an age of moral advance. Promiscuity, illegitimacy, divorce, drug-taking and crime attract a lot of attention and may well be the price we have to pay for living in a complex, mobile and highly competitive society, but they are at any time the product of only a small part of the population. If we want to talk about the moral state of our society, it is to the solid virtues of love and family life and of concern for the weak that we must give prominence.

[28] Schofield, *The Sexual Behaviour* . . ., p. viii.
[29] Fletcher, *The Family and Marriage*, pp. 208–9.

7

ECONOMIC MAN

'GIRLS TOOK PRIDE IN REPETITIVE WORK', said a headline in *The Times* on 10 January, 1963, reporting an article in *Occupational Psychology* about '400 girls employed on assembling minute electronic components'. The report went on: 'Partly because the product was important in national defence but also because of its fineness and intricacy, the girls had a sincere interest in their work and were ready to be proud of achieving high quality.' There is a widespread belief (which *The Times*, from the air of mild surprise with which it presents this report, evidently shares) that for most people work is a matter of earning money, and nothing more. This belief requires investigation.

Work

Let us take first of all the views of an industrial psychologist. Dr J. A. C. Brown, one of the leaders of this field in Britain, wrote, in 1954:

Concerning incentives in general, the following facts are significant:

(1) There is no one ideal incentive. Incentives vary from one culture to another, from one firm to another, and from one invidivual to another (e.g., one man may value money whereas another may find greater leisure or opportunity for promotion a more powerful stimulus).

(2) The law of diminishing returns applies to all material incentives – that is to say as the reward increases the desire for further reward decreases until it reaches vanishing point (e.g., as G. R. Taylor points out, the miners, on getting higher rates of pay, increased their rate of absence, because the point had been reached at which the need for more money had become secondary to the need for more leisure).

(3) Incentive may conflict with other motives (e.g., a worker may ignore financial incentives if he fears that his rate may be cut or that he may work himself out of a job).

(4) Without exception, all industrial psychologists are agreed that money is of much less significance than has hitherto been supposed. Except under conditions when wages are very low or during periods of inflation, money is one of the least powerful incentives.

(5) On the other hand, we must remember that in our own culture, as Taylor has noted, motives tend to become 'monetized'. 'People have been taught that money is the key to satisfaction, so when they feel that something is wrong with their lives they naturally ask for more money. A demand for money undoubtedly indicates that they want something, but it does not tell us what.'

. . . .

It is easily noted that, in the firm with poor morale, the workers continue to ask for more money even when wage rates are much higher than in most factories in the area.[1]

It is not easy to accept this view of the function of money in relation to work, because most of us feel money to be a major incentive in our lives, if not the major incentive. William Rees-Mogg, writing in *The Sunday Times* on September 13, 1964, just before the general election, expressed forebodings about the effects of a Labour victory on money incentives: 'There is no real prospect under a Labour Government of further incentive improvements in the rates of taxation on executive salaries. I cannot see that this taxation policy can have anything but a depressing effect on individual initiative.' Feelings, however, can be deceptive. *New Society* on 14 October, 1965, provided two quotations from speeches made by David Howells, Director of the Conservative Party Political Centre. In 1961, when the Conservative Party were in office, he said: ' . . . there is little evidence to suggest that high rates of taxation are a particular disincentive to mental effort and personal dynamism. The argument can be just as easily stood on its head with the assertion that still higher rates would induce the businessman to work harder to maintain the same living standards.' In 1965, when the Labour Party had come into office, he said: 'The maximum tax rate on individuals in West Germany is 56 per cent. In Britain it is 90 per cent. It is hard to think of a single change in Britain which would have a more dramatic climate-changing effect than an adjustment, even half way, towards the West German rate.'[2] It is no reflection on Mr Howells that these quotations contradict each other. Rather, the contradiction points to the general confusion

[1] J. A. C. Brown, *The Social Psychology of Industry* (London: Penguin Books, 1954), pp. 201–3.

[2] Quoted by Anthony King, in 'New Stirrings on the Right,' *New Society*, 14 October, 1965, p. 7.

of ideas on this subject, a confusion which all of us suffer in some degree, and it may serve to emphasize that it is worth our while to pay attention to the views of industrial psychologists and sociologists on this subject, however odd those views may seem to be.

There are three main ideas which emerge from studies of the reasons for which people work. The first is that a main objective of working is to secure an adequate money income (that is to say, an income sufficient to assure a standard of living above, or well above, the current definition of subsistence level). Lisl Klein, a research worker in industrial sociology, begins a lecture on *The Meaning of Work* by saying:

It goes without saying that the first thing that matters about work is to have it. Any discussion about intrinsic work satisfaction has to presuppose that there are no fears of large-scale unemployment, and becomes nonsense if there are such fears. The next thing, still before the intrinsic satisfaction of work matters very much, is to be adequately paid for it. To leave wages out of such a discussion is to beg another very big question.[3]

The Trades Union Congress, in its report *Automation and Technological Change*, comments on the effects of unemployment: 'Ultimately it is not merely having no work to do – important as the effect may be on a man's well-being – as having a lower or declining standard of living that is the most distressing feature of unemployment.'[4] This, like many sociological statements, may seem to be a blinding glimpse of the obvious, but it is, in fact, important for what it does not say. The acquisition of an adequate money income is not the sole reason for working.

The second idea which emerges is that when an adequate standard of living is assured, the way in which a man works is not directly related to financial incentives. Wilfred Brown, who as manager of a large works was responsible for an interesting series of studies of the relationship between incentives and work done, came to the conclusion that people tend to go by their own norm of a fair day's work and a fair day's pay:

This, then, is one of the main conclusions of my own experience with wage systems; that each individual has his own norm of pace of work and application to work and that, given a reasonable physical environment, a level of work

[3] Lisl Klein, 'The Meaning of Work', Tract 349 (London: Fabian Society, 1963), pp. 1–2.

[4] *Automation and Technologieal Change* (London: Trade Union Congress, 1965), p. 11.

reasonably consistent with this capacity and a regular level of pay consistent with such work, he will produce, on average, that quantity of work which is his own optimum contribution. He can spurt for quite short periods in emergency but he cannot keep it up.[5]

The third idea which emerges is that given a reasonable security of employment and income, the most important element in work is that it places us in the community – it gives a sense of belonging, a sense of individual value and a sense of having a contribution to make to society. Indeed, this may be the most important element even in times of insecurity; against the opinion of the T.U.C. quoted above we may set these words of William Temple: 'The greatest evil and bitterest injury of their (*sc. the unemployed*) state is not the animal grievance of hunger or discomfort, nor even the mental grievance of vacuity and boredom; it is the spiritual grievance of being allowed no opportunity of contributing to the general life and welfare of the community.'[6]

J. A. C. Brown sums up the meaning of work as follows:

(1) Work is an essential part of a man's life since it is that aspect of his life which gives him status and binds him to society. Ordinarily men and women like their work, and at most periods of history have always done so. When they do not like it, the fault lies in the psychological and social conditions of the job rather than in the worker. Furthermore, work is a *social* activity.

(2) The morale of the worker (i.e., whether or not he works willingly) has no *direct* relationship whatsoever to the material conditions of the job. Investigations into temperature, lighting, time and motion study, noise, and humidity have not the slightest bearing on morale, although they may have a bearing on physical health and comfort.

(3) There are many incentives, of which, under normal conditions, money is one of the least important. Unemployment is a powerful negative incentive, precisely because (1) is true. That is to say, unemployment is feared because it cuts man off from society.[7]

One implication of this analysis of the meaning of work is that economic activity cannot be measured only in economic terms. The economy is also human living space, and the decisions which are made within the economy must reflect this fact. Efficiency is not automatically in conflict with human considerations, but neither is it

---

[5] Wilfred Brown, *Piecework Abandoned* (London: Heinemann, 1962), pp. 93–4.

[6] F. A. Iremonger, *William Temple* (London: Oxford University Press, 1948), p. 348. The quotation was taken from a letter written in 1934.

[7] Brown, *The Social Psychology* . . . , p. 187.

automatically in harmony with them. There are, for example, some jobs, and some sorts of working conditions, which tend to create social and personal difficulties for everyone engaged in them: there is, for example, some evidence that shift-work can cause not only fatigue and physical discomfort, but also loss of interest in out-of-work activities and marital difficulties. Since shift-work is likely to be of growing importance with the spread of automation (which implies the use of continuous-flow methods of production, and an increased need to keep very expensive plant in operation for a greater part of each twenty-four hours if it is to be used to the best economic effect), the human effects will need continuous examination and continuous efforts to overcome these difficulties. Lisl Klein, indeed, advocates the deliberate creation of inefficiency on occasions, 'abandoning a technique of management practice or of production engineering, because one does not like its effects'. As she points out, efficiency is a matter of achieving certain goals, and an idea of economic efficiency which ignores the needs of the human beings who have to work the economic system may not be the right one.[8] The answer is probably to be that this is a pleasant idea, but not a practical proposition. So much the worse. If we are not willing to pay the price in this way, we shall be called upon to pay it in other ways: in divorce, in cruelty to children, in delinquency, in alcoholism and drug-taking, and in violent crime – and with these we are already all too familiar. Certainly on a Christian view of man it is our responsibility to make every effort to improve the quality of life that economic activity imposes on us; and on a Christian view of the moral structure of the world it is a responsibility that will come home to roost.

Trade Unions

In the battle to humanize economic forces the role of the trade unions is crucial. Trade unions arose in conditions of class-warfare, but as class tensions have lessened they have not disappeared, because they have a permanent function in economic life, which is to represent the interests of labour. The business of management is to take decisions about labour as a factor of production – as something that is put into the process of production and charged as a cost against the price of the product – and in taking these decisions the manager is guided by

[8] Klein, *The Meaning of Work*, pp. 20–1.

considerations of efficiency and profitability. If he is a good manager, he will also take into account other matters that affect his labour force, but even at best the welfare of the worker must be only one consideration among many that face him. Since 'labour' is also 'people', it is essential that there should be a means by which the interests of the worker as a person can be pressed against the management (if it makes what seems to be a wrong or unacceptable decision) with a force equivalent to that which the management itself can deploy – and this means is the trade union. The right-wing romantics who contrast the 'slavery' of unionism with a hypothetical 'free man' making a 'free contract' are talking nonsense, because that 'free man' never existed. Whatever freedom the worker has in industrial negotiations, he has it because of his trade unions.[9]

Does this basic task of the unions imply that a state of conflict between labour and management is a permanent feature of economic life? There are two views on this point. At the Liberal Party Conference in September, 1965, Mr David Steel, M.P. for Roxburgh, is reported to have said: 'We talk about both sides of industry when there should only be one side in industry, we talk about concessions, defeats, victories for one side or the other, we even talk about peace negotiations.'[10] He went on to advocate the Liberal policy of co-ownership. An example of the policy of worker co-operation in management is now being put into operation in Yugoslavia, where, according to an article in *The Economist*: 'Workers' decision is intended to be integral and comprehensive in industrial affairs. It governs the scope and scale of current production. It divides the surplus of an enterprise between incomes and plough-back. It has to judge the merits of new projects for expansion and amalgamation.'[11] In one factory the chairman of the workers' council is a foundry man, elected for a single four-year term. His work is described as follows:

He spends half his time in the foundry and half on workers' council affairs. There are 67 members of the workers' council, drawn from 9 departments, of whom 27 are party members. They meet formally once a month. There is also a management board of 10, half from management and half from workers, with the general manager as chairman, which meets fortnightly, apparently without formal agenda for meetings lasting one to three hours, and taking

[9] *See* J. K. Galbraith, *The Affluent Society* (London: Penguin Books, 1962), on the unions as a 'countervailing power'.
[10] *The Guardian*, 23 September, 1965.
[11] 'How Workers Manage,' *The Economist*, 16 July, 1966, p. 239.

decisions by majority vote; some go back to the workers' council for confirmation.[12]

The Yugoslav experiment is perhaps too young to carry much weight, having been begun officially in 1950 and not pursued vigorously until very recently, but the anonymous writer in *The Economist* comments:

Other visitors (British trade union leaders among them) have found much to criticise in it; this observer started sceptically, and became more impressed with what he saw. It became clear, at least, that workers' self-government provides a brand of labour relations superior to almost anything in the west or east: at any rate no false confrontation between 'owners' and 'workers'![13]

On the other hand there is the view that conflict between management and unions is a necessary outcome of economic activity. Peter Anthony, lecturer in management at University College, Cardiff, wrote in an article in *New Society* in 1965:

There *are* a variety of interest groups in most industrial situations which do not always see their long or short-term interests as coinciding. It is no service to accuracy or to improved industrial relations to ignore these conflicts or even to argue that they will be removed by better communications because they are unreal.

This is familiar ground by now. But we need to remember the role of the trade unions in this situation. If we recognise the reality of conflict in industrial relations, if, further, we recognise the social value of its controlled expression, then we must recognise the role of trade unions in organising the interest groups which they legitimately represent. The unions exist to formalise conflict in industrial relations. If conflict is not formalised then it becomes uncontrolled and uncontrollable.[14]

As industrial society is organized at present in the west, the main weight of the argument lies with Mr Anthony. In principle the interests of management and labour are not the same, and in practice conflicts do arise. The business of society is to resolve conflict, not to encourage people to slog it out, but conciliation demands a good deal of understanding and goodwill on both sides, and we cannot always count on these being present in economic life.

Strikes

The final means of resolving conflict within a particular industrial situation must therefore still be the official or unofficial strike. A strike

[12] *Ibid.*   [13] *Ibid.*
[14] Peter Anthony, ' "Responsible" Unions?' *New Society*, 16 September, 1965, p. 22.

is a trial of strength and resolution between two parties. It is not an efficient way of arriving at decisions in economic terms, but it may be highly efficient in human terms: in producing better pay or conditions, or in overcoming weaknesses in communication within the industrial situation. J. E. T. Eldridge, lecturer in sociology at the University of York, writing in *New Society*, comments:

> From the sociological point of view, the strike is essentially a breakdown in the flow of consent. It points to a problem, rather than creates one in the first instance. Unofficial strikes, particularly wildcat strikes, are usually of short duration. They certainly exercise the function of dramatically drawing attention to a felt grievance. There are at least some grounds for saying that, if it is possible to remove the source of the grievance, the effect of the strike on production will be more beneficial than detrimental.[15]

He also points out that in practical terms the distinction between 'official' and 'unofficial' strikes is not very meaningful. Whereas in the years 1900 to 1929 the average duration of strikes was 23 days a year, in the years 1948 to 1956 the duration was an average of 4·3 days a year: many strikes today tend to be on immediate and local issues which hardly give time for the often long-winded and cumbersome official procedures to be set going – and the rules of some unions are so complicated that it is difficult for them to makes strikes 'official'.

Britain is not excessively troubled by strikes in comparison with other advanced industrial nations. In the five years to 1964 the number of working days lost per 1,000 of the working population in manufacturing, construction, mining, and transport was 242 for the United Kingdom, against 32 for West Germany and 6 for Sweden, but against 302 for Japan, 352 for France, 708 for Denmark, 722 for the United States and 1,220 for Italy (International Labour Office, quoted by William Davis in *The Guardian*, 11 May, 1966). In terms of number of stoppages per 100,000 employees (all trades) for the years 1959 to 1963, the figures are (in yearly averages): Britain 10·9, Sweden 0·58, Japan 2·5, France 19·1, Denmark 1·8, United States 5·2, Italy 15·7. (Australia topped this particular table with 33·2; no figure was given for West Germany – International Labour Office, quoted by J. E. T. Eldridge in the article mentioned above.) If allowances could be made for the special factors influencing the figures for different countries (such as the influx of cheap labour into West Germany in the main post-war years, or the absence of any history of industrial bitterness in

15 J. E. T. Eldridge, 'Are Any Strikes "Wildcat"?', *New Society*, 17 March, 1966.

Sweden), the variations between the advanced industrial countries might well be less important than these figures suggest.

Some strike action is normal and even beneficial in an industrial society: it is part of the machinery of communication, and it does not produce lasting economic harm (indeed, it can make industry as a whole more efficient by forcing backward employers to pay the full opportunity-cost of their labour). Where there is a history of frequent, and long-lasting, disputes in a particular industry, this is more likely to be an indicator of deep-rooted problems (e.g., long-term decline of the industry, a history of insecurity of employment, or a long period of bad management and labour relations) in the industry, than of bloody-mindedness on the part of the unions:

> The overwhelming importance, in the roll of working days lost by strikes, of a few industries, such as coal-mining and the docks, with a long history of bad labour relations, suggests that the causes of strikes are much more to be found in the particular problems of particular industries than in general discontent with working conditions. A strike is, usually if not always, a symptom of pathological labour relations.[16]

The experiences of the acknowledged problem industries are not an indictment of the trade union system as a whole, any more than they are an indictment of management as a whole.

The major problem facing trade unions and management and government together is how to combine the legitimate workings of industrial bargaining with a situation of full employment and a tolerable degree of inflation. The orthodox counter to excessive pressure on wage-rates, which may come not only from the unions but also from firms anxious to attract and keep scarce labour, is deflation and unemployment. If a permanent state of full employment is desirable (and it may be argued that it is, from both a social and an economic point of view), some way must be found of bringing into individual wage-bargaining a consideration of the general state of the economy, and of relating increases in wage-rates to increases in both production and productivity. In spite of the crisis measures of the 1966 Prices and Incomes legislation, the main emphasis in Britain is still on voluntary restraint and the goodwill of the unions. The example of Sweden is often quoted, where wage-bargaining is closely related to national and local figures for productivity and output; but a recent study by the International Labour Office suggests that even under the

[16] D. L. Munby, *Christianity and Economic Problems* (London: Macmillan, 1956), p. 187.

most favourable conditions (i.e., no pronounced excess of demand, a willingness on the part of both unions and employers to sacrifice some autonomy in wage-fixing, and a small number of tightly-disciplined and well-federated unions) an incomes policy cannot take much strain (H. A. Turner and H. Zoeteweij, *Prices, Wages and Incomes Policies in Industrialised Market Economies*, reviewed in *The Economist*, 30 July, 1966), and there were signs in 1966 of the Swedish economy coming under strain.

When voluntary methods do not work well, there is a natural tendency to turn to thoughts of legislation, but there are difficulties about the use of the law to control labour relations. Firstly, the law is a clumsy method of settling economic questions: the use of the criminal law is plainly impracticable (what government is going to imprison, say, the entire membership of the Transport and General Workers' Union?); the use of the civil law is perhaps more feasible, but even here a determined resistance by the unions (in which, say, a refusal to pay fines by one union, leading to the imprisonment of their officials, could escalate into a general strike) could lead to economic chaos. Secondly, even if the civil law could be used without resistance on this scale, labour relationships have to be considered as a continuing activity, and the mistrust and bitterness roused by the use of the law could take years to die down, and would probably reduce the efficiency of the firm or industry in the process. Both these points were made by the Ministry of Labour in its evidence to The Royal Commission on Trade Unions and Employers' Associations (*The Times*, 3 November, 1965). J. E. T. Eldridge, in the article already referred to, points out that in the United States, where, until 1966, much more use was made of the law in labour relations than in Britain, there has been a high incidence of brief unofficial strikes with a high percentage of worker participation.

There is also a deeper objection to the use of legislation. The constant theme of this chapter has been that 'labour' is also 'people'; the trade unions are not simply part of the mechanism for fixing the price of labour, they are primarily part of the machinery of representation. Therefore an interference with them is also an interference with the process of democracy. Democracy is not always efficient, it is not always clear-sighted; but in the long run it is a lot less painful for all of us than any other method and this is as true for industrial democracy as for political democracy. If this means that we have to continue with regular doses of deflation, well, so be it, but it is not yet time to despair of finding an answer through education: the mutual education of unions and management and government in the matter of responsibility in a democratic industrial society. If at a given time there really are economic arguments for a policy of wage-restraint, and if management and government and labour are acting in good faith, it is not beyond their powers to grasp the essential facts and act upon them: but it is useless to expect such results in the absence either of good faith or of a clear understanding of the facts – which brings us to the possibilities of reform in the institutions of labour and management.

The Future of Labour Relations

The function of management being to initiate and to control, it is to management that we must first look for an improvement in labour relations. The Ministry of Labour's memorandum to the Royal Commission on Trade Unions and Employers' Associations, to which we have already referred, was reported by *The Times* to include a comment on this point:

Many disputes, the Ministry said, could probably be avoided by better and more efficient personnel management. An atmosphere conducive to strikes arose from bad communications, failure to act over workers' grievances and poor selection and training of supervisors.

'The actions of management', the Ministry said, 'not merely in the immediate case which may provoke a strike but also over a long period, can contribute to building up the power of unofficial leaders and weakening that of the full-time trade union officials. The number of unofficial disputes might be reduced considerably if the standards of personnel management were as high in industry generally as they are in the best firms.[17]

Over and over again, a difficulty in labour relations is the result of a failure to take human beings seriously. The Trade Union Congress report on technological change makes this point:

Another issue that is broader in scope than technological change is industrial democracy. Irrespective of the degree of technological advance in a particular industry or service, workers in all occupations should have the right to express views, and to have those views taken into account, about developments and issues affecting their interests. The effect of technological change is to sharpen the need. It is less than useless, and may be regarded as adding insult to injury, to go through forms of joint consultation on situations that are the inevitable

[17] *The Times*, 3 November, 1965.

outcome of decisions taken earlier by a management, perhaps at a higher level than that at which the consultation takes place. If workpeople are regarded as properly having a voice in the affairs of the nation in their capacities as voters they cannot be expected to be satisfied with no more influence than the machines in industrial affairs.[18]

When management realizes that the trade unions are a proper part of running a business, it may even come round to the idea of allowing union meetings to be held in the firm's time and at the firm's expense, as a normal part of the exercise of communication – an act of intelligence to which the unions might well respond by thinking in terms of 'plant' unions rather than 'craft' unions – or at least plant branches rather than area branches.

In this connection a particular problem is the position of the shop stewards. The research director for the Royal Commission on Trade Unions and Employers' Associations, Dr W. E. J. McCarthy, is reported to have said in a research paper presented to the Commission:

. . . from the point of view of the harassed manager, who may not have been trained to expect it, the growth of the shop steward challenge sometimes appears, at best, as interference and, at worst, as an undermining of legitimate authority. Managements could not hope to meet such a challenge without a considerable change in their previous attitudes and ways of formulating policy on industrial relations.

On the union side the challenge also presents serious problems. A union needs active and influential shop stewards to give meaning to union membership in the plant, to perform essential organisational and financial duties, and to an increasing extent to help in running the union at branch level. But there are potentially disruptive possibilities in too great a reliance on the development of semi-independent shop steward organisations.[19]

Dr McCarthy pointed to difficulties which arise from different views of what is legitimate practice on both sides, and suggested that a more systematic and planned response to shop floor demands on the part of management, more use of formal rather than informal procedures in shop-floor bargaining, a change towards basing union branch organization on the factory rather than on the place where the worker lives, the provision of more full-time union officials, and the provision of a more ready access for such officials to shop stewards in the plant would help. It was also reported that Dr McCarthy had said:

[18] *Automation and Technological Change*, p. 28.
[19] *The Guardian*, 31 August, 1966.

Since the object of changing wage structure is to make it less unstable it must be accepted that shop stewards are likely to enjoy less legitimate influence. There is thus a case for management setting out at the same time to widen the area of the legitimate negotiating rights of shop stewards by allowing them, for example, to take part in deciding matters previously regarded as exclusively managerial business.[20]

On the union side the first consideration is again communication. Whether the complaint is justified or not, one factor behind many labour troubles is a feeling that the officers of the union are not sufficiently concerned with, and aware of the thinking of, the people they represent. This is a question of both money and education. *Automation and Technological Change* makes the point with reference to both unions and management:

These references to the implications of technological changes to wages and earnings . . . emphasise the need for trade union officers to have an appreciation of the elements of costings and other management techniques as well as an understanding of the various systems affecting wages structure and earnings, or at least to have access to specialised knowledge and advice about these subjects. They all imply also that a good industrial relations climate will depend in the future on the willingness of employers to be flexible and realistic about management's prerogatives and to provide more readily the information necessary for an informed assessment of questions related to wages and earnings.[21]

There is the other side of the need for education – the capacity to deal with the complexities of modern industrial organization. If union officers are to be better trained for the job of communicating with their own members, and with management, more money will be needed for training, and more pay to attract men of the right quality into the leadership of the movement. In Sweden the Trade Union Congress receives 3/- a month for each member of the contributing unions: in Britain the T.U.C. receives 1/3 a year for each member; one West German union pays its chief 'about £5,000 a year': the general secretary of the Amalgamated Engineering Union gets '£1,750 and expenses of £100'.[22]

The other change which is surely going to be demanded of the unions by technological change is to be more flexible in their quali-

---

[20] *Ibid.*   [21] *Automation and Technological Change*, p. 23.

[22] The figure for Sweden is taken from an article by an anonymous 'Swedish industrialist' in *The Observer* of 5 September, 1965: 'Labour Relations: Have the Swedes a Secret?'; that for West Germany from an article by Peter Hordern, M.P., *in The Sunday Times* of 17 October, 1965: 'Why W. Germany is ahead'.

fications for membership and, like the American unions, to accept anyone who can do the job. The present craft apprenticeships are wasteful for those who go through them – in most trades a boy could, with proper training facilities, be a fully-trained craftsman by the age of 18 rather than 21 – wasteful in preventing the entry of older men, and wasteful in terms of demarcation disputes. As a moral question, there is a disturbing selfishness in the way some unions refuse to recognize, for example, men trained in other countries (or in prison) and in the way some unionists even today would like to expel members trained under war-time emergency schemes.

One of the most disputed questions is the right of a union to prevent a man being employed in a trade unless he is a member. The union argument is that people who work in a trade enjoy benefits secured through the union and that in fairness they should contribute to it; they argue also that where there is no closed shop the power of the unions to secure future benefits is reduced. The Ministry of Labour, in its evidence to the Royal Commission, pointed out that some employers like the closed shop in so far as it makes for easier negotiation with the labour force, and suggested that the best practical policy would be to recognize the unions' claim to the closed shop, and to provide safeguards for the individual member. This is the essential point, that in disputes with individual members the unions should not be final judges in their own cause. The Ministry commented:

This might be achieved by making union rules subject to approval by the Chief Registrar of Friendly Societies or some other independent person and by the unions setting up impartial appeals machinery for members who claimed to have suffered injustice. If they refused to do this, legislation might be considered, but powers sufficient to prevent abuses might restrict unions' essential liberty of action.[23]

The precise balance between the unions' liberty of action and the rights of individual members, given such supervisory machinery, will have to be worked-out case by case, as all political liberties are; but one right that will have to be safeguarded at the beginning is the right not to belong to a union on grounds of conscience. The number of people involved is unlikely to be sufficiently great to threaten the structure of unionism as a whole and there is no reason why such conscientious objectors should not be required to pay a sum equal to the union subscription to a charity acceptable to both sides.

[23] *The Times*, 3 November, 1965.

Whatever their faults, the trade unions have made, and continue to make, a great contribution to the quality of life in this country and it would be idle to suppose that there is going to be less need of their influence in the future than there has been in the past. The power of the unions is only one side of an equation and those who want to control the unions are noticeably less anxious to control management and finance. In the face of the forces of management and finance and government, it is not at all clear that the power of the trade unions is excessive: the unions are composed of those people who have most need to protect themselves and interference with their ability to do so would be a serious matter. The other side of this coin is that the unions should remain true to themselves. It has been the historic function of the trade unions to fight for the poor and the oppressed: it is very much to be hoped that in the future, as in the past, the unions will be able to recognize who are the poor and oppressed of today; not only the old, the fatherless and the unskilled, but also the potential new under-privileged class of British coloured people and the rising numbers of the mentally, physically or emotionally handicapped. If the unions take an interest in these, their own rights will find more supporters.

Economic Values

The activities of trade unions have to be seen in relation to the values presented by economic activity generally: it is not reasonable, for example, to blame the unions for the amount of strike action we suffer if this strike action is generated by the way in which the whole economic system works, that is, if strike action (and, in some circumstances, a high level of strike action) is simply the working-out in labour relations of a general principle of competition which is accepted (and taken to be highly desirable) in other parts of the economic process, such as the buying of raw materials, or the selling of the product.

It is a fact that in this country, although there is now more support for the idea of planning than there was formerly, and although we now have a 'mixed' economy in the sense that some industries are nationalized and all economic operations are liable to experience some form of government intervention, the main emphasis is still on competition. What is true of Great Britain is true of 'the west' generally, and the more advanced Communist economies are also finding advantages in bringing some degree of competition into their economic operations. The implications of the word 'competition' are, therefore, worth examining in some detail.

A competitive economic system is one in which prices are determined ultimately by two things: the consumer's valuation of the products (what we are prepared to pay), and the availability of resources (how much there is to go round – and there are no resources, except possibly the air over deserts and sea-water in mid-ocean areas, which are in such abundant supply that we have no need to worry about them). In a completely free price system, raw materials, labour and capital would be put into those goods and services which are of most value to the consumer (we should all get what we want most), and no product or service would use more raw materials or labour or capital than is absolutely necessary (nothing would be wasted).

A completely free and competitive system is an economist's dream and has never existed in real life, but in spite of its many imperfections, bottle-necks and sticky patches, a competitive pricing system is still the best means we have of discovering, on the one hand, how much a consumer values bread as against cake and, on the other hand, what it costs us, in terms of alternative possible uses, to put a certain amount of raw materials, labour and capital into making cake rather than bread, or supersonic aircraft rather than 'jumbo' jets. If planners were endowed with perfect knowledge not only of material resources but also of human motivation, we might conceivably do without a competitive pricing system, but until then we need it. Insofar as competition tends to reduce costs and prices, it tends to spread the world's resources efficiently.

However, this rosy picture has two less than rosy modifications to be made to it. In the first place, competition is not free, both because of the fundamental limitations of time, geography and human ability (which produce advantages for some people and disadvantages for others), and because of the fact that the most competitive way of acting is not necessarily the most profitable way of operating. Generally speaking, the consumer's interest is best served by the production of large amounts of goods at low prices, but the manufacturers' and retailers' interests may be equally well, or better, served, and with less worry, by producing a smaller amount of goods at higher prices. Although very large firms are necessary to secure economies of scale in many sorts of production (chemicals, steel, motor vehicles), when a market becomes the concern of a small number of producers the dangers of monopoly practices are always present. This is a point at which intervention by the government, which represents all of us, can be of use, and no cry about 'controls' or 'interference with business' should put us off.

The second weakness of a competitive system, left to itself, is that some aspects of consumer satisfaction (what we want) and of costs do not enter directly into the evaluations of businessmen: so, for example, a firm may be concerned with the amount and darkness of the smoke coming out of its chimneys as an indicator of how efficiently its boilers are firing, but not as an indicator of the amount of solids being deposited on surrounding housing. The 'social' costs arising out of economic activity include the effect on family life of men having to move from one place to another to find employment; the costs involved in providing new housing and services in expanding areas and abandoning housing and services already provided in declining areas; and the effect of industry on its environment, in terms of such matters as traffic congestion, clean air and what it all looks like.

One small-scale but real example of this sort of clash of interests is provided by the Derbyshire village of Buxworth where, in 1965, the brakelining firm of Ferodo were tipping asbestos waste in an old quarry. In October 1965 asbestos waste was declared to be a danger to health. The villagers demanded that the tipping, for which planning permission had not specifically been given, should be stopped. *The Sunday Times* on 14 November, 1965, reported:

> Ferodo said that the waste materials, including dust, were not pure fibre, but asbestos treated with resin. 'Processed asbestos is not dangerous to health, as far as we know.'
>
> A scientist engaged in research into the effects of asbestos said it was likely that when mixed with resin it was less penetrating or less toxic than pure fibre, but the answer was not known. 'It is undesirable anyway that people should be exposed to it.'

The answer given by Ferodo is reminiscent of a plea in court by Dorman Long, the steel firm, in a case in which they were fined £100 for 'failing to take effective measures to give warning of the approach of an overhead crane'. One man working in the path of the crane received fatal injuries. The firm pleaded guilty, through their legal representative, but, 'Mr. Taylor submitted that this was not a bad breach of the Act. He said the company paid a great deal of attention to safety and there were no fewer than five safety officers, two of whom were full time.'[24]

The gaps between the concern of Ferodo and the concern of the villagers of Buxworth, and between Mr Taylor's submission and what one might presume to be the feelings of the relatives of the dead man, are part of the difference between 'profitability' and 'social cost'. It is a difference which can be overcome only by a deeper concern, in industry and commerce, for our fellow men as human beings, and by a determination on the part of the community to see that business and industry are kept up to the mark in that concern.

The present system, in short, is one in which human interests are liable to be overridden by commercial interests, and in which human values have to be fought for. When we think of the trade unions in relation to this system, we should not overlook the fact that businesses can make unreasonable demands on management as well as on workers. The firm that requires its provincial managers to come to a meeting in London every Sunday morning may be as guilty of abuse as the firm that tries to sack an awkward shop steward. Men do not sell the whole of their lives to an employer: on the contrary, the interests of a man, his wife and children are prior to the interests of a corporation. The T.U.C. report, *Automation and Technological Change*, suggests that increasing difficulties for middle management may arise from technological change, and may point to a need for some sort of trade union activity at this level:

> Moreover, technological change is inflicting on management personnel many problems that have beset manual workers, such as redundancy, promotion and tenure, shift-work, night-work and week-end working, transferability and pay. These problems become sharper for non-manual workers as promotion prospects diminish because of the need for higher and more specialised skills. This trend emphasises the need for effective trade union organisation to deal collectively with problems that were previously regarded as issues affecting individuals rather than groups.[25]

Trade union activity is an essential part of the economic system as it exists today and as it is likely to exist in the foreseeable future. The excesses of trade union activity are themselves reflections of the competitive system and an indication of the pressures and strains which it produces.

[24] *Evening Gazette*, Middlesbrough, 10 August, 1965.
[25] *Automation and Technological Change*, p. 27.

There are many other matters in the economy which would repay enquiry: the separation of ownership from control in industry, the separation of financial control from any interest in the product or the people who make it, and the associated questions of take-over bids and rationalization procedures form an area in which current developments have some advantages to the community, but also bring with them dangers to which we have to be alert.

Enough, however, has been said to make the point that economic activity is not purely an economic matter. The economic process is important to us not only as a lot of products and services but also as a way of life, for those who work in its various manifestations and for those who have to live alongside them. Because there is a gap between what is efficient and what is humane, there will not always be easy or agreed solutions to economic problems, but economic life is part of God's creation and the demands of justice and of love must be heard in it. It does matter if steel-making produces foul air and an ugly environment as well as employment and inputs for exports; it does matter if a production process is uncomfortable or dangerous for the workman as well as cheap. The conditions with which the economy surrounds us, and the human relationships which it creates, are within our control and if the result is not as we should like it to be the fault is our own.

8

THE UNEQUAL SOCIETY

IN this study there has been occasion more than once to refer to the importance of social conditions in moral acts. Conscience itself is formed partly, if not largely, by ideas we receive from other people, and by our experience of the effects of our actions on them and of their actions on us. Crime may be the necessary result of the social stresses associated with mobility, with crowding and with competitive and acquisitive ideals of behaviour. We have noted also the way in which people acting as 'society' – that is to say, people acting in the name of all of us through various organizations, councils and ministries – may act according to a lower standard of humanity than most of us would wish to see hold good in individual relationships. All this emphasizes the fact that no social action is optional – in the sense that our choice of it arises out of our belonging to one political party or another, or our preference for one educational system or another, or our happening to be members of one social class or another – but that every social action implies a moral decision about the sort of society we want; and that the sort of society we actually produce will itself influence the moral decisions of all the people within it. It is therefore a matter of some importance that we should see what the moral issues of social policy are.

One aim that has run through all the social strivings of modern times is that of equality. As a social or political aim 'equality' does not command universal acceptance and like all great words it is difficult to define, but it has in its favour a simple theological argument which puts it at the top of the list for social guidelines. It may or may not be true that every man is equal before God – we do not know enough about God to venture to be precise about our standing with him – but it is true that the value of every man in the sight of God is so great that we cannot measure it. The value of the other in the sight of God is so great that there is no basis left to me on which I can claim to be better or to deserve more (indeed, we can claim only to be less than the other, since we are conscious of our own imperfections and weakness, but of his immeasurable value). Such an awareness of ourselves in relation to others and in relation to God is expressed in political and social terms as a desire not to treat others as less than ourselves – which is a desire for equality. The drive for equality is a drive against all those situations in which human beings suffer because they are unable to protect themselves.

Only the totally unobservant would claim that we live in an equal society at the present time, or even that we are making rapid progress towards such an ideal. In particular, there are four areas in which problems of equality arise: the areas of poverty, of colour, of education and of politics. It would need more than one book to go into these in depth, but even briefly it will be worth looking at the social facts and the moral questions which these problems involve.

Poverty

It is estimated that there are up to 750,000 children living in households with a total income below subsistence level as defined by the Ministry of Social Security.[1] Of these, some 100,000 children are victims of the 'wage-stop' – the rule by which an unemployed man is not allowed to receive more, either in unemployment benefit or in social security payments (the old National Assistance), than what the Ministry calculates his net normal weekly earnings would be if he were employed. In December, 1965, there were 16,000 families – over one third of all unemployed with children receiving National Assistance – who had their payments reduced under this rule. The system obviously hits the large families hardest, since their needs are greater: some families received as much as £7 a week less than the minimum which the Ministry itself considered necessary to keep the family going. The wage-stop applies to the long-term unemployed as well as to those unemployed for a few weeks between jobs and it applies with particular hardship to the disabled, since they tend to be unemployed for longer periods than others and their ability to earn is calculated at lower rate than that of an able-bodied

[1] Brian Abel-Smith and Peter Townsend, *The Poor and the Poorest* (London: Bell, 1965), p. 41. See also *The Circumstances of Families* (London: H.M.S.O., 1967).

man. There are also, according to Ministry of Labour estimates, between 200,000 and 300,000 families, with an average of three children each, in which the father is in full employment but has an income below the Ministry of Social Security scales; because of the wage-stop principles, these families are not entitled to help – and there is nowhere else for them to turn, except private charity.[2]

This particular failing of the social security system is one which may soon be removed, but it is worth considering as a symptom of an attitude of mind which will not be removed: 'These people are in need of help, but there is a rule against giving it.' (What is said here is not meant as an attack on the National Assistance Board staff, who as early as May, 1942, asked for an end to be put to the wage-stop system.) The reasoning behind the wage-stop ruling calls for several comments. Firstly, the intention of the rule is to prevent 'abuses' – that is to say, to prevent anyone living off the Ministry of Social Security instead of working – but the rule in effect means refusing to help many innocent people in order to avoid helping some considered to be less deserving. Secondly, the rule reveals a frightening lack of knowledge of real people on someone's part, in so far as it implies that many people would rather live off Ministry of Social Security payments than work for a living. Thirdly, it reveals an even greater lack of knowledge of the real nature of 'spongers' or 'malingerers', in failing to recognize that these are people with personality problems who are not going to be helped or even controlled by Government-enforced semi-starvation. Fourthly, it reveals a curious lack of confidence in the ability of the Ministry to sort out genuine cases of hardship from people with other sorts of trouble. Finally, it reveals a punishing attitude towards those who fail to make good which runs very deep in our society.

It is clear from the Ministry of Labour's figures that there is a substantial problem of poverty in this country (whatever the difficulties of definition of 'subsistence level') and that one cause of it is low wages; the other sources are on the one hand the effect of large families and on the other hand the traditional categories of the old, the sick, the fatherless and the widow. Each of these sources calls for a different sort of action.

Harriet Wilson, in an article in *New Society*, describes the problem of wages as follows:

Average earnings in industry are something over £18 per week. Family

[2] Adrian Sinfield, 'In Statutory Poverty,' *The Guardian*, 13 July, 1966.

allowances at present add to this 8/- for the second and 10/- for each further child; in other words they are a token contribution to total income. A man earning £18 a week who has four children may not have much more than £2 per head per week for all expenditure after insurance contributions, fares to work, rent, and expenses for fuel and light have been paid. This is hardly enough when it comes to expenditure on clothing, the replacement of furniture, or such luxuries as a summer holiday.

Half the industrial working population, however, earns less than £18 per week, and a wage of £10 to £12 per week is not uncommon in certain industries where overtime and bonus work are not available. A man with three children aged three to twelve earning £10 per week and paying a rent of £2–10–0 has a total income (including family allowances but deducting National Insurance contributions) which is £2–14–2 less than the scale rates of the National Assistance Board.[3]

The main answer here lies not so much in increasing assistance through the Ministry of Social Security as in introducing more wide-reaching minimum wage legislation. There would be a strong economic justification for this in that any business which is employing a man at a wage below subsistence level is not paying the full cost of its labour and is making an inefficient use of economic resources. Various imperfections in the labour market allow this situation to arise: lack of mobility (between locations or between trades); weaknesses of organization on the labour side; inefficient management leading to the over-employment and under-utilization of labour; and a persistent high level of unemployment in some areas – or, at least, a lack of alternative employment. This is one of the points at which some government intervention in the economy would be useful.

As Harriet Wilson's article suggests, a particularly cruel situation arises when low wages are combined with a large family. It may be a social duty in the face of world (and British) population projections to restrict the number of children in each family, but the factors which influence family size are complex and it is no answer to try to reduce family sizes by keeping large families poor: in that way we shall only create further social troubles in the future. Harriet Wilson began the article already quoted with these words:

Recent evidence shows that the large family – unless it is rich – comes off badly in almost every respect: financially in terms of income per head; educationally in terms of child development and chances of obtaining a higher education; nutritionally in terms of adequacy of dietary intake; physically in

[3] Harriet Wilson, 'The Plight of the Large Family', *New Society*, 7 April, 1966, pp. 8 ff.

terms of peri-natal mortality rates, stunted growth and height. And it is the large family that suffers most in a period of growing housing needs which are insufficiently met.[4]

Let us go into more detail on each of these points.

Diet:

That diet suffers in the households of marginal incomes is not surprising; I know many large low-income families who eat meat only on a Sunday, and then a cheap cut. A great deal of bread and jam, baked beans, and potatoes make up for the absence of animal protein. But it is more surprising to discover that the diet in large families of higher income groups suffers as well. Royston Lambert, in *Nutrition in Britain 1950–1960*, examined the dietary information published by the National Food Survey in the light of the recommendations of the British Medical Association. He found that the diet of the British people has not improved uniformly, although the nutritional situation of the nation as a whole has shown an improvement, and all social classes have shown nutritional advances. But on examining the findings by family size he found that small or childless families had made substantial gains in the decade, whereas the diet of families with three or four children had shown some notable falls in nutritional adequacy. By 1960 the families in all but the top income group were affected, and disparities of intake between families of different sizes and classes were huge. 'There is evidence', says Lambert, 'that the financial burden of a large family has increased over the decade and that the nutritional position of these groups suffered as a result of decontrol in the middle fifties. Since that time they have been unable to make up what they lost then.'[5]

Education:

It is well known that there is a negative correlation of family size and intelligence quotient of children, which is probably connected with the slower verbal development of younger children in large families. The Crowther Report produced evidence of the adverse effect of family size on the chances of a continued education: while 42 per cent of children stayed at school over the age of 15, only 8 per cent of children did so who came from families of six or more. The Robbins Report, similarly, points out that the chance of a child from a small family staying on to take A level examinations was much greater than that for a child of a large family, income and parents' educational background being held constant.[6]

Housing:

'Low income per head has a decisive effect on housing. Large families often find the rent charged for a house of adequate size too high to afford, and

[4] *Ibid.*, p. 8.   [5] *Ibid.*   [6] *Ibid.*

therefore there is considerable overcrowding in houses which are much too small. This means that children have to share beds and it is not unusual in large families that the youngest children share the bed with their parents. Sleep is disturbed and parental privacy is not maintained under such conditions. Although many local authorities operate some form of rebate scheme for rent, it is frequently the large family that owes rent. W. B. Harbert investigated the records of tenants with rent arrears in Southampton and found that 76 per cent had three children or more, as against the national figure of 8½ per cent of households containing three or more children. John Greve found that a third of London's homeless families had three or more children. At present, housing is simply not geared to the needs of the large family.[7]

On 7 November, 1966, *The Guardian* referred to a family living in three basement rooms in Westbourne Park:

They have eight children, between the ages of 5 and 18.

The flat is so damp that any covering on the concrete floors rots in a matter of months. The walls are dripping wet and full of holes and cracks and the children are not well. There is a gas stove and a point for one gas fire. There is temporary electric light because it would be too dangerous to install electricity fully. They do have a lavatory and a sink.

They have been on the housing list since 1963. They are a priority family because the public health inspector has condemned the basement as unfit. Council housing tends not to turn up for families of this size: if they split up, they would no longer be on the priority list.[8]

Obviously, the multitude of problems which faces the large family demands a multitude of answers, and one answer would be the provision by local authorities of extra-large houses at lower rents; at present the people who most need local authority housing seem to be the least likely to get it.

On diet, part of the answer lies in the continued provision of help in kind – protective foods for babies and school meals for older children. In October, 1964, only 280,000 children had free dinners, which suggests that a good many of the estimated 750,000 children of families living below subsistence level were missed out. The diffi-

[7] *Ibid*. The references here were taken from W. B. Harbert, 'Who Owes a Rent?', *Sociological Review*, XIII (1965), and John Greve, *London's Homeless*, Occasional Papers on Social Administration (London: Codicote Press, 1964).

[8] 'Challenge of Drab Discomfort,' *The Guardian*, 7 November, 1966. The article deals with the work of the Notting Hill Neighbourhood Service in trying to help families like these.

culty about any charge for welfare foods and school meals is that the disincentive is likely to operate most sharply on those who are most in need:

The consumption of protective foods obtainable at welfare clinics dropped substantially as soon as the subsidy was withdrawn in 1961. The Royston Lambert investigation showed the need for additional nutritional measures for children; therefore, the need for free school milk and a school dinner of good nutritional standard is as important today as it was in the immediate post-war era.[9]

The Plowden Report on children in primary schools notes:

The proportion receiving dinners was highest in the high social class areas where social conditions were good. It was also high where a high proportion of the working population were women. The proportion receiving milk was correlated with bad social conditions. The contrast in patterns may well have been due to the fact that a charge is imposed for meals. Thus the proportion receiving dinners tended to be low where the proportion of children in great need was high. Therefore it is likely that school meals are not being consumed by many of those who are in most need of them. Survey research is needed to investigate whether this is so.[10]

This section of the Plowden Report ends with the general comment that 'The distribution of educational resources is not highly correlated with social conditions which generate needs for them, and the same is true for other social services for children.'[11]

Clearly, if British entry into the European Common Market is followed by a rise in food prices – and an eventual rise of up to 25/- per week for a small family is suggested by some economists – one result will be a further lowering of the nutritional standards of the poorest.

On education, the answers will include nursery schools and play space to remedy the lack of attention and stimulus given to the under fives in large families, play areas for older children, and substantial maintenance grants for children taking higher education between the ages of fifteen and eighteen.

On financial help in general, the most favoured suggestion (which

[9] Wilson, *New Society*, 7 April, 1966, pp. 8 ff.
[10] Central Advisory Council for Education (England), *Children and Their Primary Schools*, the Plowden Report, II: *Research and Surveys* (London: H.M.S.O., 1967), Appendix 14, 'Notes on Variation in L.E.A. Provision', para. 14, p. 625.
[11] *Ibid.*, p. 630.

may well be put into action shortly) is to abolish the tax allowances for children (which are more help to those with higher earnings, and no help to the poorest), and to increase substantially the family allowances. All these ideas call for more money from general taxation; but they might well justify themselves, even in strictly economic terms, by producing a better-trained and more stable labour force, a lower rate of delinquency, and fewer demands on the National Health Service. It may seem odd to justify compassion in economic terms, but in a world created by God it is encouraging and not unexpected to find that the action dictated by love also tends to be the most efficient (though not necessarily the cheapest) action.

The third source of poverty is the traditional poor: the old, the chronically sick, the fatherless and the widow. Unless furnished with a private income, anyone who falls into any of these categories (except a widow who is qualified and able to work) automatically drops down to the lowest standard of living considered tolerable in our society – and that level, as we have noted already, is usually below any reasonable definition of 'subsistence' level. No one becomes sick or fatherless willingly, or out of idleness. It ought to be possible now at least to see that the old do not starve or freeze to death, that children do not have to stay at home because they have no shoes, that those who need extra milk and eggs can afford them. Yet in 1966 none of these things were assured to the poorest. This cannot be entirely because of the poverty of the nation, since we are now able to arrange matters so that a man out of work receives a benefit related to his previous earnings instead of a flat rate (again a measure which automatically excludes the poorest from any benefit), and so that a man made redundant receives a cash payment related to his period of service. These are both useful measures – but meanwhile the very poor stand and wait. Perhaps here again we are up against an attitude of mind. It is not only financially that the traditional poor suffer. *The Guardian*, in an article called 'Ghetto for Artisans' on 30 August, 1966, describing the Manchester overspill estate of Hattersley, had the following passage:

Those who suffer most are the old. One old woman was recently moved from a furnished flat in Hulme to a Hattersley flat; she was left without furniture for several days when she had to dine and sleep off packing cases. Another old woman did not receive a single visitor in her first six months on the estate, apart from tradesmen and the rent collector. A third old woman, a chronic invalid, was moved into a Hattersley flat without any notification being sent to Welfare authorities at the Hyde end. She was only found a few days later, her packing cases unpacked (*sic*). Within two days she was dead.

It would need another book to detail all the disabilities from which the poor suffer, but across all of them there lies this thought: it is not the means to help that is lacking, but only the will.

It is worth noting that, despite superficial impressions to the contrary, the system of taxation in Britain since 1938 has not led to any substantial redistribution of income. Although rates of taxation are officially very high, the possibilities of altering the basis on which income is taxed (by such means as covenants to other members of the family, the spreading of income over retirement through insurance policies, and the use of expense allowances and benefits in kind) are so many that the proportion of real income which bears tax is greatly reduced. At the same time there has been a switch in fiscal policy from taxation which varies according to income (mainly income tax) to flat-rate taxes (such as national insurance and health service contributions) which has increased the relative burden of taxation on the poorer part of the community. A careful analysis has been made of the effects of taxation policy by Professor Richard Titmuss in his book *Income Distribution and Social Change*. In the course of this study Professor Titmuss describes the conclusions reached by J. A. Brittain in an article on 'Some Neglected Features of Britain's Income Levelling' (*American Economic Review*, Vol. L, No. 2, May 1960, p. 596):

(Mr Brittain) started with the original pre-tax statutory distributions, and made adjustments for missing investment income and undistributed company income including stock appreciation, but not of capital appreciation. The result of these exercises showed no levelling of pre-tax income between 1938 and 1949 and 'a remarkable stability in the inequality measure' over the whole period 1938–55.

On the basis of these measures, he then proceeded to consider the effects of fiscal redistribution. Taking the Blue Book incomes after direct taxes, he made adjustments for imputed 'social service' benefits (education, health and housing expenditures and food subsidies), missing investment income, and post-tax undistributed company income. As a result of these calculations, 'the 1949–55 interval shows a 4 per cent rise in inequality, and the over-all 1938–55 decline is more than halved. In sum, the official figures exaggerate the over-all levelling and hide a clear reversal of the trend after 1949'.

Mr Brittain concluded that 'there is no convincing evidence of a "natural" levelling' since 1938. The income 'revolution' which did occur (attributable almost wholly to changes in the top 2 per cent of incomes) 'was a largely inadvertent or accidental by-product of the high taxes, subsidies and dividend

E

restraint required to finance the military budget without runaway inflation' during the war, and since 1949 it has been clearly reversed.[12]

Professor Titmuss himself concludes:

> Whatever else may be said about the criticisms we have made about the sources of information and about those who have interpreted the material, there can be little dispute with the conclusion that we know less about the economic and social structure of our society than we thought we did.

It follows from this that we should be much more hesitant in suggesting that any equalizing forces at work in Britain since 1938 can be promoted to the status of a 'natural law' and projected into the future. As we have shown, there are other forces, deeply rooted in the social structure and fed by many complex institutional factors inherent in large-scale economies, operating in reverse directions. Some of the more critical of these factors, closely linked with the distribution of power, and containing within themselves the seeds of long-lasting effects – as, for instance, in the case of settlements and trusts – function as concealed multipliers of inequality. They are not measured at present by the statistics of income and only marginally by the statistics of wealth. Even so, there is more than a hint from a number of studies that income inequality has been increasing since 1949 whilst the ownership of wealth, which is far more highly concentrated in the United Kingdom than in the United States, has probably become still more unequal and, in terms of family ownership, possibly strikingly more unequal, in recent years.[13]

The pressure for relief from taxation, and the ever-present sense that welfare has 'gone far enough' always threaten the well-being of the poor. In the end this is a political problem, and it is as a political problem that we shall return to it at the end of this chapter.

The question of the relationship of our standard of living to that in other countries is so large that we cannot begin to deal with it here; but any society which lets a large gap appear between rich and poor is heading for trouble, and this is as true between nations as within nations. Indeed, the trouble has already arrived, for the 'Communist threat' in the east is as much an economic as a political problem; we, however, prefer to regard it as first of all a military problem – perhaps from a delusion that military problems are more easily soluble than others.

Colour

The problem of poverty is traditional, the problem of colour is quite new, at least for this country and in the particular form in which

[12] Richard Titmuss, *Income Distribution and Social Change* (London: George Allen & Unwin, 1962), p. 139.   [13] *Ibid.*, p. 198.

we have it now. It has always been the tendency among us to resent the foreigner and the immigrant, whether he was a Jew or an Irishman or a Pole or a Hungarian, but today, for the first time in history, we have to face the fact that – without desiring it and without realizing it – we have become a multi-racial state. For the first time we have an immigrant element which is not only substantial and permanent, but also easily and permanently marked out because of its colour. The most serious social question facing us in the next twenty years is whether it is going to be possible for coloured people to live on equal terms with white, above all in housing opportunities and in job opportunities; and in a longer period, whether we shall be able to begin to regard the colour of a man's skin as little as we now regard the colour of his hair.

Immigrants, whether coloured or white, do not in themselves constitute a problem. They do not necessarily have a higher proportion of delinquents, of unemployables, of bad housekeepers or of disease than comparable sectors of the host community: bad housing, problem families, delinquents and unemployables were all known in Britain before the immigrants arrived. Irish immigrants, now largely absorbed into the general population, were at first described in the same terms as can be found today being used of coloured people, such as 'dirty', 'lazy', 'trouble-makers' and 'ignorant'; again, in 1904 there was an agitation for laws to control and reduce the immigration of Jews from modern Poland and the Ukraine, not unlike the agitation which led to the current immigration legislation.[14] The difficulty which faces us now is that even if the coloured people wish to be absorbed into the general population (and there is no particular reason why they should), they will continue to present a simple visual identification which can all too easily attract the fears and resentments of the host community: a 'black' who can be blamed for all our troubles. The existence of such stereotypes is probably unavoidable so long as we have troubles to project. What can be avoided is the practice of discrimination on the basis of colour by employers, landlords, public servants and public entertainment enterprises.

[14] William H. Israel, *Colour and Community – A Study of Coloured Immigrants and Race Relations in an Industrial Town* (Slough Borough Council, 1964), p. 5. William H. Israel is the General Secretary of Slough Council of Social Service. The book is now out of print. The notes on Jewish immigration were taken from: N. D. Deakin, 'Immigration and British Politics,' *Crucible*, May, 1965, pp. 80–6. *See also* the issues of January and March, 1967. *Crucible* is a magazine published by Church Information Office.

Where discrimination does operate, the result will be that the coloured population will tend to get the worst housing, the worst schooling, and the least chance of employment – in fact, they will become the major group at risk for every social disability. The result could, in the long run, be violence. The explosive potential of an underprivileged group who are clearly identifiable to themselves and to others by the colour of their skin has been amply demonstrated by the riots in some cities in the United States (for example, in the summer of 1966). It could happen here, and in a very few years. *The Times*, in a series of articles at the beginning of 1965, under the title 'The Dark Million', estimated the present coloured population at about 800,000; on the basis of the people already in the country it has been estimated that by 1970 one school leaver in six in Birmingham may be coloured, and that in Bradford by the same date one in four of new-born babies may be coloured (such estimates are no more than guesses, but even if they exaggerate the situation they do give some indication of the size of the problem).

Britain is not a tolerant nation. Surveys differ widely in the precise degree of colour prejudice they discover, but there is good reason to suppose that 'a mild antipathy towards coloured people and a tendency to avoid too intimate a social contact with them is virtually a cultural "norm" in Britain'.[15] In a survey in Slough, whereas over 90% of Indian, Pakistani and West Indian workers interviewed felt that they 'get on well with British workers around you (them)', only 26%, 20% and 35% respectively felt that they had 'the same opportunities for advancement and promotion'; on the other hand, 131 out of 165 thought they had made a wise decision in emigrating, and in a survey taken among members of the host community 68% of the people replying selected terms favourable to the immigrants in a question in which they had to choose from paired favourable and unfavourable terms.[16] A survey in which 272 Jamaicans were interviewed first before leaving Jamaica and again two years after arriving in Britain

[15] Deakin, *Crucible*, May, 1965, pp. 80–6. Mr Deakin also quotes two surveys, one in 1951 by 'a well-known research organisation' which was interpreted to mean that about one third of those questioned were actively prejudiced against coloured immigrants, and one in 1956 by Dr Michael Banton, who found 10% of his respondents prejudiced and 76% neutral. *See also* Clifford Stanley Hill, *How Colour Prejudiced is Britain?* (London: Gollancz, 1965) which suggested that only 10% are not prejudiced on the question of intermarriage, but has been criticized both for the small size of the sample and for the framing of the questions.
[16] Israel, *Colour and Community*, pp. 58, 75, 89.

showed that they tended to find their way into the lower-paid jobs in the lower-paid industries, and suffered much more from over-crowding than the average for the country as a whole, and that they tended to stay socially within their own racial group; but also that there was little tension arising between black and white in industry.[17] It should be noted that people from the West Indies generally find it easier to settle in Britain than people from other parts do – as the Slough survey by William H. Israel also showed.

The immediate need is obviously for measures of practical help to newly-arrived immigrants, assistance to schools by quota systems and special language classes, and the provision of interpreters and liaison officers wherever there is an immigrant community; there is need also for the watch-dog work of the race relations board, and for legislation against discrimination (though it is not easy to draft laws against discrimination which do not run the risk of infringing the liberty of the citizen in general – we have a long history of laws being used for purposes which their originators never intended). But the long-term answer lies not in special measures for coloured people, but in a large programme of action against social disabilities in general. Any government now that sits lightly to questions of bad housing, poor schools, lack of industrial training facilities, un-employment and run-down medical services will be contributing to racialism as well as to poverty and delinquency. Firm action in the negative sense, against discriminatory practices, and in the positive sense, to encourage the idea of racial unity through the way other countries are presented in schools, and through the way race relations are handled in all the communications media, can back up such a general social policy, but are not a substitute for it.

The problem of colour is a problem of justice, but it is also a problem of love. Equality in housing, equality in jobs are important because they affect people's feelings, because they are part of the way in which we accept or reject one another. As one man wrote about his son, serving with the British army in Aden:

Perhaps they will listen when I tell them about the boys and girls, the young men and women, sons and daughters of immigrants. These young people who have all the entitlements of citizenship, but no assurance of belonging. Because the limbo into which they were born has no length or breadth,

[17] R. B. Davison, *Black British Immigrants to Britain* (London: Oxford University Press, 1966).

no geographical location or definition. Because each day of their lives is a confrontation with the frightening, inescapable question of identity.

Even when enjoying the advantage of citizenship. Even when fulfilling the responsibilities of citizenship.

Am I or am I not a Briton?[18]

It is important for the sort of place that Britain is to be, and it is important for the sort of people that we are to be, that we should give the right answer to that question, and that we should give it in actions rather than in words.

Education

We have to deal with another sort of segregation when we come to consider education. The educational system is in the middle of a period of rapid change and the main directions of the change are becoming clear: the trend towards comprehensive schools, the trend towards doing away with ability streams, and the trend towards planning the teaching programme around what the child wants – or needs – and around group work and learning by doing, rather than formal teaching. These are trends which many people find disturbing, but it is at least arguable that these actual and impending changes are helping to make a more responsible and tolerant society.

What should we want for our children? That they should find themselves accepted and acceptable, that they should learn to live with their fellow men, and that they should develop their own interests and abilities as far as they wish. None of these objectives is fulfilled by the educational system as it has been up to the present time, with its emphasis on the idea of 'ability' to the exclusion of almost all else.

So far from accepting the children entrusted to it, education, pursuing the idea of the 'ability stream', has worked by a process of systematic segregation. At every level the children have been sorted out according to 'ability' – by 'streaming' in the primary schools, by separation at the secondary stage into different kinds of school – grammar, technical and secondary modern – and by 'streaming' again within these schools. Further education also has been divided between those who do not receive it (or receive it only part-time), those who go to local authority colleges (technical colleges and colleges of education), and those who go to university. For the majority of children, who are of average or below average ability, the main

[18] E. R. Braithewaite, 'Outsider,' *The Guardian*, 11 October, 1965.

experience the educational system has provided has been that of being rejected – in slow stages.

Alongside these educational divisions, and operating separately from them, has been a social division arising from the tendency of people of different social levels to live in different geographical areas. It is sometimes claimed that the division into different types of school is valuable precisely because it tends to cut across this social/geographical division, but the strong link between social class and educational ability means that in effect 'grammar' tends to equal 'middle class', and 'secondary modern' to equal 'lower class'.

The system of segregation has a second effect, which is to reduce the chance of children learning that the differences between human beings are less important than the things they have in common, because the system itself implies that the community is fundamentally divided into two or three kinds of people.

The third effect of the concentration on the idea of ability is that the system has not allowed each child to develop his abilities to the full – his feelings, his imagination, and his creativity, as well as his capacity for rational thought. A programme which followed what the child wanted to do rather than imposed what we think the child ought to be doing would be a horrifying thought to people of a controlling and punitive turn of mind, but the alternative – and what, in fact, the present system does – is to regard the human being primarily as an information store. We are, in fact, quite good information stores (some better than others), but this is not our most important ability, even when we are thinking in terms of education. The worship of 'academic ability', which underlies both the system of segregation and the system of examinations, necessarily leads in a false direction, because it elevates to the first rank a quality which is at best of second or third rate importance in human life and it causes a great deal of harm in so doing.

The comprehensive principle in primary and secondary schooling is sufficiently well established on educational grounds to need no further argument here.[19] It does, perhaps, still need to say that a comprehensive school needs a comprehensive set of buildings designed for the purpose; that a wide geographical separation of parts of a school makes nonsense of the whole idea; and that the utilization of old buildings by the invention of an intermediate school for eleven

[19] The arguments are set out by Robin Pedley, *The Comprehensive School* (London: Penguin Books, 1966).

to thirteen year olds does no good to anybody except, in the short run, the ratepayers. But even a genuine comprehensive school in new buildings under one administration, serving all the secondary age group in an area, does not in itself solve all the problems of equality and opportunity, for there remains the question of 'streaming'.

Streaming is the division of the children in an age group into classes according to an ability test – and the similar sub-division of them within classes. There are strong educational arguments against this practice. J. W. B. Douglas, in an investigation of nearly 1,000 children in the primary school years, has found evidence that streaming significantly widens the gap between children of upper and lower ability ranges in the course of their time in the primary school.[20] Professor Thelen of the University of Chicago in an article on streaming in *New Society* made the following points:

A great deal of research has been done to compare the achievement of children grouped homogeneously (streamed) according to ability with children in the old fashioned heterogeneous (unstreamed) classroom groups. And all the research (Eckstrom, Drews, Borg, Passow – to name the better studies) reached the same conclusion: the case for homogeneous ability grouping is *inconclusive*. Name any measurable educational objective you like and the chances are equally good that students grouped heterogeneously will gain more on it than students grouped homogeneously.... *Within* a heterogeneous class, subgroups composed *ad hoc* of those students who are 'ready' for a particular activity – such as a reading exercise over certain words – seem to work very well. But note that these groupings are determined by the activity, and that they are reconstituted quite regularly on the basis of careful assessment of what sort of experience each child will profit from. This is the principle of the ungraded classroom, and its success will depend on the ability of the teacher to set up a variety of different kinds of activities, and on the ability of the teacher to assess the strengths and weakness of students almost daily.[21]

Brian Jackson, director of the Advisory Centre for Education (an offshoot of the *Which* consumer research organization), in a comparison of ten primary schools using streaming with ten unstreamed schools, found:

[20] J. W. B. Douglas, *The Home and the School* (London: MacGibbon & Kee, 1964). This is the third stage of a follow-through study of 5,000 children born in the first week of March, 1946. The previous volumes are *Maternity in Great Britain* and *Children Under Five*. See also *The Flexible School*, a supplement to *Where*, published by the Advisory Centre for Education, 57 Russell Street, Cambridge.

[21] Herbert A. Thelen, 'To Stream Or Not to Stream?', *New Society*, 25 February, 1965.

There was not the drive, competition, or tension in unstreamed schools common in the streamed schools; more time was devoted to music, art and drama, and rather less to the desk-work of arithmetic and English exercises. The teaching techniques were usually different – with less class work, and much more small group and individual work. They were schools in which children frequently *surprised* their teachers by some new interest or success.[22]

It was more difficult to compare the academic results in the two sets of schools, but:

. . . there were eight cases where the reading progress of a year group of streamed children could be compared with a year group of unstreamed children. Two of these comparisons showed little difference between either method. The other six follow the pattern reported in previous research by Dr. J. C. Daniels: *all* children improved somewhat in the unstreamed schools, but the weakest children gained most. Besides creating higher academic standards, unstreamed schools had a narrower spread of attainment. The long 'C' stream tail had disappeared.

There certainly were considerable *social* differences between them. Unstreamed schools replaced competition by helpfulness. For example, in most of the streamed schools it was an offence for one child to turn to another for aid with an arithmetical problem. This was 'copying' and to be punished. Yet in most of the unstreamed schools this turning of one child to another was constantly encouraged by the teachers.[23]

A preliminary report from the National Foundation for Educational Research on its investigations into the organization of Junior Schools and into the effects of streaming forms Appendix 11 of the Plowden Report: *Children and their Primary Schools* (II, Research and Surveys, pp. 544–94). The results of this survey so far are 'of dubious validity' because they are not yet based on the follow-through of one group of children from the beginning to the end of primary education and therefore the present findings involve comparing different children at different ages, but the preliminary conclusion is that as the results stand 'they lend small support to controversialists on either side'[24] (p. 576). The report shows significant differences in attitudes between teachers in streamed and non-streamed schools: the climate in non-streamed schools tends to be 'more permissive and tolerant, less structured and places less emphasis on the more traditional methods of class teaching than its streamed counterpart'.[25] The survey suggests

[22] 'Streaming: an Education System in Miniature', *The Observer*, 15 November, 1964.
[23] *Ibid.*   [24] *Children and their* . . . , II, p. 576.   [25] *Ibid.*, p. 558.

that the attitudes of the teachers, in both sorts of schools, may be more important than the formal organization: 'The interviews and visits to schools suggested that teachers in streamed schools differed from those in non-streamed schools, both in their teaching methods and in their attitudes. It also became clear that these differences between teachers in their methods and attitudes might possibly outweigh the effects of streaming *per se.*'[26] In the conclusion to this section the report states:

 . . . (the results) also indicate that the effects of teachers' beliefs and attitudes are to be looked for not so much perhaps in differences in formal attainments as in children's beliefs and feelings about themselves and their underlying attitudes to school and what it stands for. It is not in the nature of cross-sectional evidence to throw much light upon questions such as this, though we may hope that something will emerge from the follow-through study. One point does, however, seem to be clear. A mere change in organization – the abandonment of streaming, for example – unaccompanied by a serious attempt to change teachers' attitudes, beliefs and methods of teaching, is unlikely to make much difference either to attainments or – though this is less certainly based on the present evidence – to the quality of teacher-pupil relationships.[27]

Again, an investigation into the effect of teachers' attitudes on pupils leads to the conclusion that ' . . . the more important and far reaching effects of streaming or non-streaming lie much less in formal attainments than in the human and personal aims of education'.[28]

The survey of Junior School organization casts doubt on the efficiency of selection into streams:

After the initial assignment to a class or stream in the first year of the Junior school, the chances of a pupil being transferred are very slight.

Taking the school year 1961–62 as a typical year, it appears that movement between streams was relatively small. Once children had been assigned to their streams at seven-plus most of them would remain in the same stream throughout the four years of the junior school. Against this we should put Vernon's estimate, based on the known correlations of the measures used, that about 10 per cent of all children should be upgraded or downgraded each year if relative homogeneity is to be preserved.

Thus reliability and validity of the methods used for grading children to A, B or C streams when they first enter the junior school appear to be of the utmost importance; it is surprising to find that so many junior schools graded their pupils without the help of standardized tests and without making allowance for age. Since the same largely unscientific criteria as are used to grade the

26 *Ibid.,* p. 556.   27 *Ibid.,* p. 576.   28 *Ibid.,* p. 581.

children initially are also used to assess whether second, third or fourth year children should be regraded, it is hardly likely that grading errors will be recognized and rectified at these later stages. Lack of transfers could, of course, be due to an accurate assessment at seven plus, or could be a result of a self-fulfilling prophecy in that membership of a stream tends to condition learning.[29]

The other problem that remains is that of examinations. The usefulness or otherwise of examinations is not yet being argued so widely as that of streaming, but two points can be made. The first is that, as is well known, the marking of examination papers is unreliable. Sir Alec Clegg, Chief Education Officer of the West Riding County Council, in an article in *New Society*, quoted an experience in his own area:

Recently the headmaster of Otley Grammar School put 28 pupils in for the English Language O level examination under two different boards. These were not borderline candidates. In one case, 27 passed and one failed; in the other, three passed and 25 failed. In the one case, the average grade was 4; in the other, it was 8. Two candidates only out of the 28 were placed in the same grade by both boards, and one candidate was placed in the top grade by one board and the bottom grade by the other. This is not an isolated case, nor confined to one subject – though it is interesting that the case I quote is English Language, the one subject which is regarded as so essential for so many purposes.[30]

Uneasiness about examination marking is reflected in the tendency towards the alternative answer system, in which the candidate merely marks one of a number of possible answers printed on the paper, but this system is of limited application and raises considerable problems in the composing of examination papers. It is very difficult to devise an 'open-ended' examination that will give full play to an 'open-ended' candidate, as against one who has thoroughly learned his material with this examination (and perhaps this examiner) in mind; this is a difficulty which persists right through the system at least to the university first degree examinations.

Examinations are not really necessary either for educational institutions' own use or for the use of employers. It is not necessary for students to be graded for the internal purposes of a school or college: what the educator needs to know is what a student is interested in and how to bring that interest on. It is not necessary for employers to

[29] *Ibid.*, p. 551.
[30] Alec Clegg, 'Education: Wrong Direction?', *New Society*, 11 February, 1965, p. 20.

have prospective employees graded by their school or college: what
the employer needs to know is what course the student has followed
and what work he has produced. A portfolio of essays would be of
more real use than a degree parchment (the problem of the authenti-
cation of such material is not insuperable). If the employing organization has neither the knowledge nor the time to read such a portfolio,
it probably does not need to know how good the student is. A similar
view was put forward by Dr John Morris, lecturer in Occupational
Psychology at the University of Manchester, in an address to businessmen, according to a report in *The Guardian*, which attributed to him
the view that very few paper qualifications guarantee that a person
has current knowledge or technical skills: they might show past
achievements, but rarely indicate a capacity for growth; consequently,
firms should not take university degrees uncritically, but use them as
a starting point during interviews.[31] When it is considered that a
medical student may have had four tries at an examination, and that
until the regulations were changed recently a bar student might have
had seventeen or more tries at an examination, it may be seen that
there is some point to these remarks.

Even if these two purely educational problems, of streaming and of
examinations, could be sorted out, two social difficulties underlying
education would still remain. The first is the relationship between
'ability' and social class. J. W. B. Douglas noted in his *The Home
and the School* in relation to streaming that there is a higher percentage
of the children of professional and managerial workers in the upper
stream, than the measured intelligence of the children would have
led us to predict, and Brian Jackson says, 'It was clear that streaming
worked as a major form of social as well as academic selection.' Sir
Alec Clegg, in the article already referred to, says:

If you look carefully at the Registrar General's classifications and then at the
Scottish survey of the distribution of intelligence published some years ago
you will not be able to obtain accurate figures, but the approximation at
which you will arrive is that the white collar workers, who make up 20 per
cent of the population, produce 40 per cent of the brightest children, who then
secure 60 per cent of sixth form places and 80 per cent of university places.
Conversely, the manual workers who, because they outnumber the rest by
four to one, produce about 60 per cent of the ablest children, secure only
20 per cent of the university places.[32]

[31] *The Guardian*, 11 November, 1965.
[32] Clegg, *New Society*, 11 February, 1966.

Clearly, a number of factors are working against the brighter child from poorer parents; and the same factors are also working against the less able child from the same sort of background.

The second social difficulty is that the comprehensive school, in removing educational segregation, risks reinforcing social segregation, in so far as most of its children will come from the same geographical area, and will therefore (at least in large centres of population) tend to be of the same social group, thus perpetuating and sharpening the divisions that already exist in society. It could mean also that schools in underprivileged areas would become underprivileged schools (something that already happens to secondary modern schools). To some extent this effect might be avoided by consideration of this factor in the placing of new schools, and by the drawing of the zones from which each school draws its pupils, but there are often practical difficulties in the way of both these remedies.

The cumulative effect of the present system of education is that the children who need the most help are those for whom we in fact do least, from birth to adult life. As Sir Alec Clegg, in the article already referred to, again says:

The Newsom report is a major documentation of the fact that the children born into the worst homes are brought up in the worst schools. Let us take a cold look at what we do to the weaker Newsom child. We say: You have not been selected at 11 for the grammar school. You are not good enough for the GCE stream in the modern school. You are not even good enough for one or two CSE subjects in the modern school. You will, therefore, be placed in one of the forms which gets the poorest teachers, the least choice of subjects, the most meagre use of facilities, the least homework, and whose members assume the least responsibility and are the first to be sacrificed when teachers are absent. When you leave you cannot train as an apprentice. According to Henniker Heaton, you will be the last to secure day release. You will be the last to be cared for by the industrial training board.

This is bad enough, but the other day I was talking to the managing director of a large and very well known firm. He is a sensitive and concerned person and he told me that there was no place in his firm for juvenile operatives. Most of the unskilled work was now done automatically and what wasn't was given to adults. He said that he will in the fairly near future need all the trained employees he can get, but he cannot train them in anticipation as union rules will not allow it. He can only train one apprentice to every four operatives. Yet as we recall at Rochester in the United States when the riots occurred there were 3,000 vacancies for trained men and 7,000 untrained men, mostly juveniles, who could not fill them.

And with this savage problem before us we are for the next ten years going to spend our substance in the secondary schools on examining the average child. It is not Robbins, but the CSE, which will drive out Newsom, and we shall still go on wondering why it is that some teenagers behave as they do, why Clacton and Margate occur, and we shall blame the youngsters and not ourselves.[33]

Equality in education is not a matter of levelling down – or of levelling up – but of giving each the chance to find the level he or she really wants to work on. It is a matter of seeing that every child who enters the educational system is of the same importance as every other child and deserves the same attention, the same amount of skill, and the same scale of facilities. It is a matter of giving outward form to the belief that levels of ability and levels of attainment are not themselves of the first importance, but that the kind of people we are helped to become is of the first importance.

Politics

Most of the problems raised in this book involve political action, and in particular the problems of inequality do so. It is therefore worth considering, finally, whether these problems point to a particular sort of political action, or to action through a particular political party.

In general, the answer is probably 'No'. Christian comment is not bound to any party or section of interest; it does not speak unanimously for the right wing or for the left wing, for the younger generation or for the older generation; on the contrary, it tends to crop up unexpectedly and to point in unexpected directions; its distinctive mark is (or should be) that it demands to be accepted or rejected according to the moral quality of the message (and the speaker). This is an uncomfortable demand in politics, which deals (rightly) in words like 'practical' and 'acceptable' and 'interest', and there is consequently a fairly constant desire among politicians that the church should not interfere in politics; but because it is widely recognized that it is part of the church's job to comment on what goes on in society, the rebuke is often put less bluntly: it may be said that the comment is 'inopportune' or 'unfortunate' or 'not well founded' – and sometimes, of course, it is not well founded, but the job of making comments remains a valid one.

[33] *Ibid.*

When, however, we come to the question of inequality, there is a difference between the two major parties in Britain, which makes one of them closer to the Christian position than the other. For the Conservative Party (at least at the present time) concentrates on the interests of the 'pacemakers' in society – the rising young executives, salesmen, scientists and technologists who are reckoned to set the pace in expansion and change – rather than on the interests of those who most need help. Francis Boyd, the political correspondent of *The Guardian*, commented on the 1965 Conservative Party conference:

> The Conservatives plan to finance reliefs to pacemakers in part by the transfer of more of the cost of social services from the Exchequer to the employers and by a new system of agricultural support in which the consumer will pay more and the Exchequer less. The Exchequer might thus afford more tax reliefs. This opens a more spacious future for the pacemakers (and for all other income tax payers); but several millions of income earners pay no tax at all either because their incomes are below the tax level, or because they are entitled to reliefs which exempt them from tax. How would these people benefit from concessions to pacemakers, and how in fact can a pace be set which the rest are sure to follow?[34]

He concluded:

> Liberal proposals for partnership may, or may not, be the magic that does the trick. Labour's dream of a more equal society may not prove powerful enough to carry all the pilgrims over their long and flinty road. But Liberals and Labour see the political problem in broader terms than those which were emphasised in Mr. Heath's policy statement last week. It may be that the Conservatives, in trying to egg on the clever, the ambitious, and the thrusters, are not only undervaluing a sense of common purpose in the public, but running the risk of injuring the rest who constitute by far the larger part of the community.[35]

It is not that those who are concerned for the pacemakers have no concern for the needy, but that the order of priorities which puts concern for the pacemakers first is very different from the Christian order. The claims of equality are fundamental, and if those who suffer from inequalities are relegated to one department, one section of interest, this is almost as bad as disregarding them altogether, because it shows that the real meaning of our life together in Christ has not been understood.

[34] Francis Boyd, 'How Conservative Is Mr Heath?', *The Guardian*, 12 October, 1965.
[35] *Ibid.*

For once in a while it is possible to make a clear moral distinction between the two parties in this one respect; doubts may be generated by the Labour Party in other directions, but on the point which has concerned us in this chapter, the concern of society for the poorest, for those who are being hurt, it is the Labour Party which still fulfils its historical function of being the party of social conscience.

The final implications of the relationship between social conscience and political parties may well be wider than this, because there are signs in all parts of Christendom of a reawakening to the political left which may be the beginning of a reassertion (long overdue) of an important strand in Christian tradition: the connection of social concern with radical politics. In this light, the beginning of the dialogue with Marxism by the Roman Catholic Church and other churches could be the opening of an entirely new chapter in Christian social thinking and social action.

9

THE FREE SOCIETY

The ideas put forward in this book are neither revolutionary nor impossible to carry out. Indeed, in some respects they are rapidly being overtaken by public opinion and even by legislation. If some of the points made here still cause a sense of outrage, those who are upset may care to ask themselves how much fuss and what dire prophecies were made, for example, about Roman Catholic emancipation and about universal suffrage – yet no great disasters followed these two reforms (they may, of course, also comfort themselves with the thought that the rightness of reformers on those two subjects does not guarantee the rightness of modern reformers in their own proposals).

The value of a proposal for reform, or of any comment on any aspect of society, depends first of all on how far it is based on an appreciation of the facts and it is difficult, if not impossible, to become an expert in as many fields as this book has entered, so that the opportunity for mistakes has obviously been very large. Nevertheless it has seemed worth while attempting to comment on a wide range of social activities because the changes in our understanding of man and society which are coming from the social sciences, the biological sciences and psychology, as well as from the new directions in theology and biblical studies, affect everything that we do and we have to live out the questions that they raise even if we do not understand them.

Secondly, the value of any comment on society depends on the value of the general principles by which the judgement is made. There are many possible views of the world and this book is written from within one of them, which is Christianity. The Christian faith is about the relationship between God and man and about the principles on which that relationship is based; and from there it is about the relationship between man and man and about the principles on which that relationship is based; and these principles are love and reverence. Love means that any hurt suffered by one human being is the concern of all human beings; as Paul says in his letter to the people in Galatia: 'There is no such thing as Jew and Greek, slave and freeman, male and female; for you are all one person in Christ Jesus' (3.28). Reverence means that we have to treat our fellow men as trustworthy – at least as trustworthy as we are ourselves. Are these principles valid?

Any declamation of the general principles of Christianity can be expected to draw polite murmurs of approval, but the difficulty comes in attempting to follow them. Despite our intellectual concern with love and justice and despite our emotional involvement with the needy and helpless, we do not always succeed in love and reverence for humanity; we are often not as good with our own family as with the suffering Vietnamese, not as good with children who hurt animals as with animals that have been hurt, not as good with the criminal as with the victim of crime, not as good with the racist as with those he seeks to rule. What holds up our application of love and reverence to everybody may be the fact that we do not apply them to ourselves. Jesus of Nazareth said 'As the Father has loved me, so have I loved you' and he added 'Dwell in my love' – not for cosiness but because, as his follower John said, 'Perfect love banishes fear' (John 15.9–10; I John 4.18). Before we can be free in our dealings with others we must be free in ourselves; to exercise tolerance demands the courage first of all to accept ourselves. We are not free automatically: feeling hurt by someone, we wish to hurt others; insecure in relation to the forces within us and around us, we seek safety in controlling others; not accepting ourselves, we find others unacceptable. The courage to accept ourselves – and others – cannot be found within ourselves: it comes only when we find ourselves accepted by someone greater than ourselves, namely, God. 'It is by this that we know what love is: that Christ laid down his life for us' (I John 3.16). It is possible to use Christianity as an institution for a retreat from tolerance – to take refuge in the assumed anger of God against the things we fear – but this is not what the Christian faith is. It is also possible to take refuge from the demand for real tolerance and courage by refusing to take part in the institutional church – to have high ideals but not to put them to the hard test of working with our fellow men (who are frightening because they are at bottom a mirror of ourselves) – but this also is not what the Christian faith is.

Man can be free – but only in community: in community with

God and in community with man. It is the business of society to be the place where love is worked out in this double relationship. It is the business of society to be the place where every human being can find out what he is and what he is capable of becoming and where he can find out what others are and what they are capable of becoming. It is the business of society to be the place where we can find out that every human being, whatever his failures, is a 'Thou' and not an 'It'. There is a very large gap between what society can be and what it is: industrial squalor, the tendency to an authoritarian approach, the admiration for competitiveness, and the failure to make use of those means of understanding one another that we already have, all make our society something much less than desirable. But we have to start somewhere, sometime. It might as well be here and now.

ACKNOWLEDGEMENTS

MANY people have contributed to the making of this book: in particular the people of Pallion, Sunderland, and Gordon Hopkins, their Vicar; Miss Amy Buller, M.B.E., and Anthony Bland, the Principal of St Catherine's, Cumberland Lodge, Windsor, where much of this book was written, and the people of Acaster Selby with Appleton Roebuck, where it was completed.

I am indebted also to those who have given permission for the use of published material, in particular to *New Society*, *The Guardian*, *The Observer* and *The Times* for extensive quotations; to *The Economist*, *The Listener*, *The Sunday Times* and *Nova;* and to the following publishers for permission to quote from the works listed:

Bobbs-Merril Co., Inc.: Joseph Butler, *Fifteen Sermons*, 1952
Helicon Press: Maurice Villain, *Unity*, 1963
Little, Brown & Co.: Michael Schofield, *Sociological Aspects of Homosexuality*, 1965.
University of Toronto Press: Richard M. Titmuss, *Income Distribution and Social Change*, 1962.

July, 1967   MICHAEL KEELING

BIBLIOGRAPHY

1. What do Moral Statements Mean

Bowman, A. K., *The Life and Teaching of Sir William Macewan*, London: Hodge, 1942.

Flew, Anthony and MacIntyre, Alasdair (eds), *New Essays in Philosophical Theology*, London: SCM Press, 1955.

Polyani, Michael, *Science, Faith and Society*, London: Oxford University Press (for the University of Durham), 1946.

Ramsey, Ian T. (ed.), *Christian Ethics and Contemporary Philosophy*, London: SCM Press, 1966.

Ross, Sir W. David, *Foundations of Ethics*, London: Oxford University Press, 1949.

Waddams, Herbert, *A New Introduction to Moral Theology*, London: SCM Press, 1964.

2. The Sources of Christian Moral Judgements

Buber, Martin, *I and Thou*, Edinburgh: T. & T. Clark, 1937.

Butler, Joseph, *Fifteen Sermons*, London: Bell, 1952.

The Little Flowers of St. Francis, London: Dent, 1963.

Hoyle, Fred, *The Nature of the Universe*, Oxford: Blackwell, 1957.

Orwell, George, *Nineteen Eighty-Four. A Novel*. London: Secker & Warburg, 1949.

Sayers, Dorothy, *The Mind of the Maker*, London: The Religious Book Club, 1942.

Tillich, Paul, *The Courage To Be*, London: Nisbet, 1952.

Villain, Maurice, *Unity*, London: Harvill Press, 1953.

3. Human Responsibility

Brown, J. A. C., *Freud and the Post-Freudians*, London: Penguin Books, 1961.

Fordham, Freda, *An Introduction to Jung's Psychology*, London: Penguin Books, 1959.

Julian of Norwich, *Revelation of Divine Love*, London: Methuen, 1927.
Mairet, Philip, (ed.), *Christian Essays in Psychiatry*, London: SCM Press, 1956.
The Nature of Stress Disorder, Conference of the Society for Psychosomatic Research May 1958, London: Hutchinson Medical Publications, 1959.
Philp, A. F., *Family Failure*, London: Faber & Faber, 1963.
Ramsey, Ian T., (ed.), *Biology and Personality*, Oxford: Blackwell, 1965.
Tauler, John, *The Inner Way*, London: Methuen, 1903.

4. The Criminal Law

Devlin, Sir Patrick, *The Enforcement of Morals*, London: Oxford University Press, 1959.
Gardiner, Gerald, *Capital Punishment as a Deterrent and the Alternative*, London: Gollancz, 1956.
Hart, H. L. A., *Punishment and the Elimination of Responsibility*, London: The Athlone Press, 1962.
Klare, Hugh J., *Anatomy of Prison*, London: Penguin Books, 1962.
Miller, Derek, *Growth into Freedom*, London: Tavistock Publications, 1964.
Church of England, *Punishment*, London: Church Information Office, 1963.
Radcliffe, Lord, *The Law and Its Compass*, London: Faber & Faber, 1961.
Report of the Committee on Homosexual Offences and Prostitution (the Wolfenden Report), London: H.M.S.O., 1957.
The Royal Commission on Capital Punishment (report), London: H.M.S.O., 1953.
Home Office, *The Sentence of the Court*, London: H.M.S.O., 1964.
Walker, Nigel, *Crime and Punishment in Britain*, Edinburgh: Edinburgh University Press, 1965.
Wootton, Barbara, *Social Science and Social Pathology*, London: Allen & Unwin, 1959.

5. The Right to Life

Abortion, London: Church Information Office, 1965.
Decisions about Life and Death, London: Church Information Office, 1965.

Ministry of Health, *Deformities Caused by Thalidomide*, London: H.M.S.O., 1965.

St John-Stevas, Norman, *Life, Death and the Law*, London: Eyre & Spottiswoode, 1961.

Williams, Glanville, *The Sanctity of Life and the Criminal Law*, London: Faber & Faber, 1958.

6. Men, Women and Children

Bovet, Theodore, *A Handbook to Marriage and Marriage Guidance*, Longmans, Green & Co., 1958.

Fletcher, Ronald, *The Family and Marriage*, London: Penguin Books, 1962.

Hegeler, Inge and Sten, *An ABZ of Love*, tr. by David Hohnen, London: Neville Spearman, 1963.

Oliver, J. R., *Pastoral Psychiatry and Mental Health*, New York: Charles Scribner's Sons, 1932 (out of print).

Schofield, Michael, *The Sexual Behaviour of Young People*, London: Longmans, Green & Co., 1965.

———————————— *Sociological Aspects of Homosexuality*, London, Longmans, Green & Co., 1965.

7. Economic Man

Automation and Technological Change, London: Trades Union Congress, 1965.

Bagrit, Sir Leon, *The Age of Automation*, London: Penguin Books, 1966.

Brown, J. A. C., *The Social Psychology of Industry*, London: Penguin Books, 1954.

Brown, Wilfred, *Piecework Abandoned*, London: Heinemann, 1962.

Galbraith, J. K., *The Affluent Society*, London: Penguin Books, 1962.

Iremonger, F. A., *William Temple*, London: Oxford University Press, 1948.

Klein, Lisl, *The Meaning of Work*, London: Fabian Society, 1963.

Mott, Paul E., and others, *Shift Work: the Social, Psychological and Physical Consequences*, London: Cresset Press, 1965.

Munby, D. L., *Christianity and Economic Problems*, London: Macmillan, 1956.

Tawney, R. H., *The Acquisitive Society*, London: Bell, 1952.

J. M. Todd (ed.), *Work*, Downside Symposium No. 3, London: Darton, Longman & Todd, 1960.

8. *The Unequal Society*

Abel-Smith, Brian and Townsend, Peter, *The Poor and the Poorest*, London: Bell, 1965.

Children and their Primary Schools, A report of the Central Advisory Council for Education (England) (the Plowden Report), I: Report; II: Research and Surveys. London: H.M.S.O., 1967.

Davison, R. B., *Black British Immigrants to Britain*, London: Oxford University Press, 1966.

Griffith, John, *Coloured Immigrants in Britain*, London: Oxford University Press, 1960.

Half Our Future, A report of the Central Advisory Council for Education (England) (the Newsom Report), London: H.M.S.O., 1963.

Israel, William H., *Colour and Community*, Slough Borough Council, 1964 (out of print).

Jackson, Brian, *Streaming*, London: Routledge & Kegan Paul, 1964.

Miller, T. W. G., *Values in the Comprehensive School*, London: Oliver & Boyd, 1965.

Pedley, Robin, *The Comprehensive School*, London: Penguin Books, 1966.

Tajfel, Henri, and Dawson, John L., (eds), *Disappointed Guests*, London: Oxford University Press, 1965.

GENERAL INDEX

Note: This Index does not include the main headings given
in the table of contents.

INDEX OF BIBLICAL REFERENCES